Crosscurrents / MODERN CRITIQUES

Harry T. Moore, *General Editor*

Tycoons and Locusts
A Regional Look at Hollywood Fiction of the 1930s

Walter Wells

WITH A PREFACE BY

Harry T. Moore

SOUTHERN ILLINOIS UNIVERSITY PRESS
Carbondale and Edwardsville

FEFFER & SIMONS, INC.
London and Amsterdam

For Joan, Tony, and Chris

Library of Congress Cataloging in Publication Data

Wells, Walter, 1937–
  Tycoons and locusts.

  (Crosscurrents/Modern critiques)
  Bibliography: p.
  1. American fiction—Hollywood, Calif.—History and criticism. 2. American fiction—California, Southern—History and criticism. 3. American fiction—20th century—History and criticism. 4. Hollywood, Calif., in literature. I. Title.
PS285.H6W4   813′.5′209   73–4266
ISBN 0–8093–0606–9

Contents

The title of Walter Wells's book, Tycoons and Locusts, alerts
the potential reader. Of course the book is about Hollywood
writers; the reader will be pleased to note that Dr. Wells
essentially deals with his subject as a form of regional writing,
which he carefully defines and usefully discusses. He de-
liberately doesn't go beyond the 1930s, though in briefly
mentioning some of the later variants of what he calls "Southland" writing, he shows a thorough awareness of the post-
thirties developments. He doesn't choose, however, to draw
out the discussion to include later authors who followed the
earlier trends of comic irony and "the perversities and unrealities of the place." He is content to give us a fresh look
at the writers who were in Southern California at the time of,
or a bit earlier or later than, Nathanael West's The Day of
the Locust, which came out in 1939, the year before he died,
and F. Scott Fitzgerald's The Last Tycoon, which he left unfinished at the time of his own death in 1940.

Those two books are, in any event, the California master-
pieces of that decade. West and Fitzgerald are among the
really first-class novelists who wrote screenplays, sometimes in
disastrous attempts, particularly painful in the case of Fitzgerald. The latter was dealt with, as a character, in Budd
Schulberg's novel, The Disenchanted (1950), a pretty poor
novel. But Schulberg has been consistently overrated, and it's
good to see that Walter Wells doesn't really contribute to
this activity. When a small section of Schulberg's What
Makes Sammy Run? came out in Story Magazine in the late

thirties, it seemed bright and well put together; the novel of that name, published in 1941, was simply too long drawn out to justify the space taken up by an extended anecdote. Yet, as I said, Professor West doesn't overrate the book; he speaks twice of Schulberg's "flaccid narrative," and that really describes one of the main difficulties in reading it.

The author of this book also treats Raymond Chandler, whom most of us are willing to accept as a lightweight who is at least interesting to read. James M. Cain is somewhat more serious and also interesting. Walter Wells additionally discusses John O'Hara's Hope of Heaven (1938), which is one of the few really good novels written by that excellent short-story writer who too often tried and failed at the longer form.

The author ends with a chapter on Fitzgerald, "The Hero and the Hack," in which he makes a statement, about The Last Tycoon, to the effect that "its first-person narrative by Celia Brady is clearly its most serious flaw"—right enough, but we must remember that the book was left unfinished; and it is the kind of judgment no one could safely apply to Nick Carraway's first-person narrative in Fitzgerald's The Great Gatsby. Dr. Wells also discusses The Pat Hobby Stories, those rather rueful tales of Fitzgerald's years of Hollywood tribulation, and finds the stories "hurried fictions which bear the scars of deadline." He notes, however, that they are "nonetheless illuminating from our special critical standpoint, that of the relationship between fiction and place." True; but I'd like to close this particular discussion of The Pat Hobby Stories with the last paragraph of my review of those tales, for the Saturday Review, when they came out in 1962: "Here a major talent, forced into minor writing, turned out better work than minor talents capable only of minor writing." And again—one word more—Walter Wells has given us a fine survey of the field he undertakes to study, and the value of his book is increased because he is not merely writing sociohistory, but literary criticism.

HARRY T. MOORE

Southern Illinois University, Carbondale
February 22, 1973

Acknowledgments

I wish to thank the following publishers and agents for allowing me to use quotations from their books:

From *The Postman Always Rings Twice*, by James M. Cain, copyright 1934 by James M. Cain. Copyright renewed © 1962, 1964 by James M. Cain. Reprinted by permission of Alfred A. Knopf, Inc.; and also by permission of Jonathan Cape, Ltd., the British publisher.

From *They Shoot Horses, Don't They?* by Horace McCoy, copyright 1935, 1963 by Horace McCoy. Reprinted by permission of Harold Matson Company, Inc.

From *Hope of Heaven* by John O'Hara, copyright 1938 by John O'Hara. Reprinted by permission of Random House, Inc.; and also by permission of Faber and Faber Ltd., the British publisher.

From *The Day of the Locust* by Nathanael West, copyright 1939 by The Estate of Nathanael West. Copyright © 1966 by Laura Perelman. Reprinted by permission of New Directions Publishing Corporation; and also by permission of Laurence Pollinger Limited, Author's Agents.

From *Farewell, My Lovely* by Raymond Chandler. Copyright, 1940, by Raymond Chandler. Reprinted by permission of Alfred A. Knopf, Inc., and Hamish Hamilton, London.

From *What Makes Sammy Run?* by Budd Schulberg. Reprinted by permission of Ad Schulberg.

From *The Last Tycoon* and *The Pat Hobby Stories* by F.

Scott Fitzgerald; reprinted by permission of Charles Scribner's Sons.

From *The Bodley Head Scott Fitzgerald;* reprinted by permission of The Bodley Head.

Introduction

Though the fiction of Hollywood in its fictively most productive period is the dominant interest of this study, the book was born out of a broader curiosity. I wished to probe the relationships and interactions between literature and place —the old and currently unfashionable concept of literary regionalism. Much has been said over the years about those relationships; indeed, published commentary on literary regionalism is voluminous. Yet little of it, for reasons chapter one examines, could be considered by the aesthetically oriented critic to be at all definitive, or even very useful. It is this gap in understanding which the present study was intended to narrow. After bringing the problem of literary regionalism into focus, its opening chapter attempts to offer a critical formulation, one more illuminating than any heretofore available, of the influence of place on serious literature. Thereafter, with that formulation as hypothesis, the book turns its attention to a body of fiction which at first glance seems to possess some degree of unity attributable to place, a body of work which *in toto* we are only beginning to explore —the fiction associated with the Hollywood–Southern California milieu of the 1930s.

Those critics who have earlier turned their attention to that fiction have given substantial impetus to the work at hand, work which hopefully advances theirs. My acknowledgments in this respect are owed most to Frederick Bracher's *American Quarterly* examination of California writers from a regional perspective, to Carolyn See's unpublished encyclopedic treatment of Hollywood fiction, to the late Edmund Wilson's critiques of the boys in California's cultural back room, and to Franklin Walker's indispensable surveys of the early literatures of San Francisco and Southern California. In the preface to his Twayne study of James M. Cain, David Madden refers to "detailed similarities" in the work of Cain's Hollywood contemporaries which go beyond the scope of his study. Those similarities, in their extent remarkable perhaps even to those who have noted them, are precisely the scope of the present study. With a regional hypothesis of some refinement in hand, the book proceeds, after its opening chapter, on the double mission of exploring an exciting body of fiction, and through that exploration affirming the critical usefulness of the regional idea. For those more interested in the fictions themselves than in the regional idea which informs my treatment of them, the book may start slowly. Hopefully the treatments though, generated as they are by that governing perspective, will reward these readers for their patience.

Given this twofold mission, the book becomes one of close reading and explication, never ranging too far from the books which constitute its primary focus or from their place of origin. In witnessing various patterns of consistency and recurrence, the study returns repeatedly to many of its earliest observations. In one respect, the book's focus is also somewhat parochial, beginning with a look at the American manifestations of an idea not uniquely American—that of literary regionalism—and concentrating thereafter upon an even more limited patch of literary geography. But its motives are broad. Besides seeking, and uncovering I think, some genuinely new insights into the fictions themselves, it also argues, by implication, a much wider applicability of the regional idea. Hopefully, the book will encourage acceptance of that idea as a tool for obtaining new and critically useful insights into fictions far afield from Hollywood.

My sincere thanks go to Jay Martin for his perceptive critiques of my opening chapter and the chapters on John O'Hara and Nathanael West. My thanks as well to colleagues David Rankin and Abe Ravitz for their readings of that opening chapter, and especially to John Whitley of the University of Sussex for the many hours out of a busy schedule he afforded the entire work. Some of the thinking of my seminar students is reflected in the chapters on O'Hara and Schulberg, especially that of Jane Phillips and Louise Shammas. I am grateful to each, and each is of course exonerated from any complicity in the study's faults.

WALTER WELLS

Irvine, California
November 1972

Tycoons and Locusts

1

The Regional Perspective and Hollywood-Southland

The idea of literary regionalism has never held still beneath the glass. At times, as in the respected 1938 cross-disciplinary study of American regionalism by Howard Odum and Harry Estill Moore, it has been confirmed "a fact and reality beyond question." [1] Though Odum and Moore only quickly gloss the literary landscape, their tone is clearly intended to settle the long-standing matter once and for all. Two years later, however, forsaking the gentility commonly ascribed her adopted region, Marjorie Kinnan Rawlings could call the very idea of literary regionalism "glib . . . false and unsound . . . an ill-assorted mating of concepts and [at that] . . . not even a decent bastard." [2] So much then for settled matters. Though unequivocal, neither pronouncement offers much to illumine the relationships between place and letters. Taken together, though, they do give us some idea of the limits and, for the most part, the tenor of nearly two centuries of dialogue on literary regionalism.

While any attempt analytically to subdivide an idea risks oversimplification, it helps if we view the idea of belletristic regionalism as the object of two divergent kinds of interest: that of the literary historian and that of the critic. Most of the debate over regionalism down through the years (and only recently subsided) reflects a failure of this or that commentator to heed this fairly obvious distinction. That poets and fiction writers have often focused upon and drawn inspiration from region is indisputable; that reviewers and other literary tastemakers have fostered these links is no less so. This is enough for historians, who proceed from there to trace and assess the influence of these impulses upon a literature, and to explain their historical significance and their relationship to other ideas and impulses. Critics, on the other hand—though usually in terms more circuitous—ask essentially "so what?" Their concern, rightfully, is with the extent to which, if at all, these verifiable impulses give aesthetic shape to a work of literature, to the corpus of any one writer, or to the body of writing we tend to associate with a region. Unlike the historian, the critic does not assume that mere links warrant his attention. He asks what difference it makes that the work of art before him, or that which seeks his sanction as art, is identifiable with some patch of geography. He asks, too, in what ways the artist's use of region enhances his art, or in what ways, precisely, one's intimate knowledge of region sheds critical light on the art identified with it. While skeptics like Marjorie Rawlings have insisted that the very idea of literary regionalism corrupts our tastes and undermines our values, wiser and more cautious critics like Frederick Bracher have viewed the regional idea more as testable hypothesis than unquestionable fact, or unmitigated bunk. The critic must, of course, be prepared to assume the historian's perspective: the historical ebb and flow of an idea are one dimension of that idea's pertinence to any work. And the historian need be prepared at least to acknowledge, if not to satisfy, the critic's questions, lest his own historical assessments of that ebb and flow lack aesthetic relevance. But the two kinds of interest are distinguishable and, if we are to probe the idea's usefulness—as we shall—need to be distinguished from one another.

It is evident, as one reads through the voluminous commentary on the regional idea in American letters, that the historian's perspective has produced a far more illuminating body of insight and analysis than that of the critic. Writers like Carey McWilliams, Benjamin Spencer and, more recently, Jay Martin, with historical perspectives of varying breadth, have given us a clear picture of the regional idea's genesis and progress.[3] Spencer's view of the idea's cyclical progress through five distinct phases is indispensable. Critics' views, though, and the critical statements of writers themselves on the links between place and literature, have accumulated into a mass of confusing abstraction, contradictory assessment, and unsubstantiated pronouncement. Mary Austin's oft-quoted remark is typical: to be genuinely regional, she has said, a work must be *of* and not merely *about* a region.[4] Her definition enjoys aphoristic conciseness, but the distinction she makes (besides echoing one made by William Gilmore Simms a century earlier) is far too vague a base for the critic to proceed from in assessing the aesthetic influences of place upon writing. Even Bracher, who acknowledges the confusion surrounding the regional idea, does little to allay it. Though expressly preferring that the concept be treated hypothetically, he leaves the problem essentially untouched (as, to be fair, most other critics have) by offering no hypothesis sufficiently refined to allow for serious testing. Bracher speaks instead of a "*sense* of identification" between a region and a work, a sense which he feels "is hardly demonstrable or analyzable [but] must be felt." [5] Certainly, if a regional perspective is critically at all worth assuming, it must provide more than mere stimulus for intuition.

So the questions are these: Can the critic go beyond intuition, past the welter of contradictory assertion, to question productively the "regionality" of literature? Is the concept of literary regionalism at all valuable to the critic? and if so, to what extent? Such sweeping questions are rarely answered once and for all—Odum, Moore, and Rawlings notwithstanding. This study aims at no such finality. One of its outcomes is, though, I think, some measure of increased clarification of the regional idea from the literary critic's point of view. Before the chapter is out, a regional hypothesis sufficiently refined for critical application will be posed. Thereafter, from this regional perspective we will look closely at a body of fiction which, superficially at any rate, exhibits a degree of unity attributable to place: that fiction generally associated with the Hollywood–Southern California milieu of the nineteen thirties. The results are not only some interesting insights into the works themselves and a clearer sense of the relationships between them (which prove far

more than superficial), but also affirmation of the regional
idea's critical usefulness.

First, some order needs to be made out of the mélange of
definitions and designations which have accumulated around
that idea. The terms *region* and *regionalism* do indeed, as
Donald Davidson has said, lose all exactness when they enter
the literary vocabulary.[6] Early on, the term *regionalism* was
used (to cite but one of a number of hazy distinctions) as
both synonym and euphemism for *sectionalism,* a term more
current in literary circles before the Civil War. Henry Seidel
Canby, whose *Saturday Review* was major forum during the
question's heyday in the 1930s, used the two terms indistinguishably. At the same time, however, Robert Penn Warren was calling regionalism "a more polite expression than
sectionalism," a "somewhat disinfected" label for the cultural centrifugality which, in politics, had torn the nation
asunder within living memory.[7] During the young nation's
quest for literary independence in the early nineteenth century, regionalism (née sectionalism) was looked upon, variously, as the best (or only) path to a great national literature,
as a more attainable goal than a great national literature, or
as a pallid substitute for one. Regionalism has also, at times,
been used synonymously with *localism,* and at other times
as its antithesis, suggesting not only some far broader slice
of terrain but an attitude stridently antilocalist. Eudora
Welty uses the terms interchangeably, while ardent localists
like Joel Chandler Harris (who see man's spiritual roots in
the isolated village or bend in the road), and staunch regionalists like Ellen Glasgow (who deride the "superficial
picturesqueness" of the localists) both maintained the distinction with some belligerence.[8]

Such varying and often contradictory usages make it ad-
visable for the critic, in any attempt to define and apply the
regional notion, to forego specifying how large or small an
area of influence need be. What at first might seem like
hypothesis-building by default is simply to dispose of an
historically persistent but critically insignificant factor. If
critically significant relationships between place and literature
do exist, why demand that the place be either large or small?

The place need only be compassable by the artistic sensibility and possess some unifying set of indigenous characteristics worth encompassing. Tentatively, then, literary regionalism can be seen as a concept which supposes some significant relationship between a geographical place—its history, its geotopography, its institutions, or its collective mentality—and the literature of that place. What remains to be defined, or course, is *critical significance.*

Toward this end, one further set of distinctions must be drawn, self-evident distinctions but ones which have nonetheless been blurred. They are distinctions between various *degrees* of regional involvement in a work. These distinctions give us categories by no means as rigid in practice as in theory, and they do help to bring the question of regionality into sharper focus. At the most superficial level, region may, as Mary Austin has pointed out, be used merely as backdrop for a narrative just as well told against some other setting. (I am reminded here of a "creative writing" teacher I know who advises his students "if you want to write a story of mystery and intrigue, and location doesn't matter, set it in Istanbul. Get your landmarks and street names from Arthur Frommer," he tells them, "and your readers will eat it up!") It is safe to assume that the narrative whose setting is mere convenience or connotative tickle is not likely to display many critically significant relationships between place and literature.

At a second level of involvement, region supplies not only backdrop but inspiration. The library shelves of many an antiquarian society creak under the results: fictional and poetic ephemera intended primarily to celebrate a place, books which adoringly exploit a region's "romantic past," its folklore, its mythic qualities, its stereotypes, its "color"—in short, its cherished clichés. Helen Hunt Jackson's *Ramona* and the "historical" fictions of Stewart Edward White are prime Californian examples. They are fictions in which, as Scott O'Dell once observed, "there is always a surfeit of flashing eyes, swishing fans, castanets, and jingling spurs." [9] No more than mere backdrop involvement do these superficialities of region warrant the attention of serious critics.

A third level of regional involvement can, for lack of a better term, be identified as documentary regionalism, literature which takes as its subject the more complex realities of a place, and as its intent a serious and truthful portrayal of those realities. A number of nineteenth-century California travel narratives and diaries do precisely this—those of Richard Henry Dana, "Dame Shirley," William Manly. When such works are accorded the stature of serious literature by critics (the term *minor classic* is a favorite) it is usually for reasons of candor, style, and the elemental quality of their central conflicts—reasons which bear only minimal relationship to the place in question. The regional elements of such works can be extremely fruitful for anthropologists and historians, but are usually of little special interest, as such, to the critic.

Finally there is that level of regional involvement which goes beyond backdrop, romance, and documentation into the area of legitimate critical concern. Begging its validity for the moment, we can call this level that of aesthetic regionalism, that degree of involvement in which specific and discretely identifiable characteristics of region can be seen informing the very qualities of a work which give it claim to the status of art, those qualities which justify the interest of the critic in the first place. Formalist criticism has pretty well spelled out those qualities for us: the vividness of a writer's sensory appeal, the originality of his motifs and his metaphor, the genuineness of the tensions and conflicts which impel his narrative, the uniqueness of his characters, the acuity of his point of view, the quality of the correlatives with which he reinforces his themes and reflects his attitudes, the appropriateness and impact of his style, the cohesiveness of his structure, and the success with which he brings all these qualities to bear upon a significant theme and a central conception. If and when these aesthetic dimensions, any or all of them, are informed by region, then region necessarily becomes of interest to the critic. If the critic is fully to understand fiction which is thusly informed, he must account for the informing elements of region and their aesthetic relationship to the work under scrutiny.

Regionality in a work of literature is neither vice nor virtue. Those proclamations of its intrinsic value found in countless articles, forewords, and literary society addresses have understandably fueled the contempt of generations of critics; most of them are unbearably puerile. Many critics, however (granted with reams of regionally inspired ephemera in mind), have argued the converse just as carelessly: that regionality in itself is an aesthetic liability. It is neither. From any sensible standpoint, regionality must be viewed as a wholly neutral factor, as a disinterested measure of the relationship between place and literary effort. That relationship may exist in greater or lesser degree in any work, and contribute with varying degrees of success to the work's aesthetic achievement. Undisposed either for or against regionality, the critic must be prepared not only to demonstrate the single incidence of regional influence, but to measure *how* regional a work is, and how aesthetically successful that regionality. He must also pursue regionality beyond the single work; presumably, all of a writer's work involved with a certain region will show unifying effects attributable to it. Presumably, too, different writers who draw with regularity upon a region will show some unifying threads attributable to it. Were this not so, discussion of "Southern regionalism," "New England regionalism," and the like, would be critically worthless.

Admittedly, this constructing of a regional hypothesis is abstract and syllogistic—useful as a starting point, but in need of application if its value is to be demonstrated. Before we apply it, though, several ancillary questions must be disposed of. There is, for one, the idea that to be significantly regional a writer must be born in, or at least have spent his formative years, within the region, preferably with his roots going back generations into the region's past. It is a simplistic and distracting demand, one which Bracher dismisses by pointing out that Robinson Jeffers, with unchallenged credentials as a literary Californian, was a native Pennsylvanian, while Robert Frost, so much a part of the New England tradition, was a native Californian. What counts is that a writer, whatever his regional tenure, know the region intimately, and that this intimacy find its way into the aesthetic makeup of his writing. The fact that most "Hollywood" writers never do come to feel at home in Hollywood is a basic factor in their fiction.

Another point to be clarified is that literary regions exist in time as well as space. Those regional characteristics and idiosyncrasies capable of informing literature can change with time. That the present-day South, for example, is different from the antebellum South is self-evident, different not only in the sum total of its history and its social mentality but—thanks to factors like industrialization, urban growth, and TVA—different in geography as well. This raises a question of the regional writer's use of the past. Margaret Mitchell, writing *Gone With the Wind* in the 1930s, was in many respects writing of a region different from her own. The Yoknapatawpha of Faulkner's *Sound and the Fury* is, in the same respects, different from the Yoknapatawpha of *The Unvanquished*. Both *Gone With the Wind* and *The Unvanquished*, in their use of place, draw upon regions partly beyond the reach of their author's perceptions. As a consequence, the two works tend to retreat into what I have called romantic regionalism—a dependence upon the historical stereotypes and clichés of place. Scott Fitzgerald, working on the screenplay of Mrs. Mitchell's novel, thought the book good but not very original because it leaned too heavily upon the Southern myth and offered "no new characters, new techniques, new observations—none of the elements that make literature." [10] Irving Howe has similarly observed that the historic South of *The Unvanquished* remains "a muted shadow, a point of reference rather than an object for presentation, perhaps because the effort to see it in fullness would be too great a strain on the imagination." [11] The intimacy with region aesthetically demanded of the writer by our hypothesis can no more be temporally than spatially second-hand.

In the best of several earlier studies of the Hollywood genre (and its most comprehensive), Carolyn See defines the Hollywood novel as "an extended work of fiction set in Hollywood which includes at least one major character or several minor ones working in show business, or . . . any novel of the American film industry on location so long as the action of the book focuses on motion-picture making and the lives of motion picture people" [12] —a definition few would quarrel with. The term *Hollywood*, nominally a geographical designation, long ago became metonymy for the motion picture industry (though the industry almost as long ago overspilled Hollywood's actual boundaries); hence the acceptability, from one standpoint, of defining Hollywood fiction as fiction about the industry. But where does this leave the critic in search of aesthetic insight, the critic less concerned with fictional subject matter, per se, than with the ways that subject matter is or is not transmuted into art? For him, Miss See's definition is but another in a long line of subgeneric categories imposed upon fiction, and of little value.

The first hint to emanate from our regional hypothesis is that the notion of Hollywood fiction as related solely to the motion picture industry may, from any critically significant standpoint, be too narrow a view. If place is at all informing and shaping a body of literature in southern California, then the motion picture industry may be but one of a number of informative regional elements, perhaps a major factor in one novel, and a minor factor, perhaps no factor at all, in another. Most of the historical, geophysical, and sociopsychological characteristics that are Hollywood's—even the industry itself—are those of a wider geographical area: of the city of Los Angeles (of which Hollywood is a part), of Los Angeles County (of which the city is only a part), and of the entire coastal and inland area of southern California (of which Los Angeles County is but a part). If place is indeed an aesthetic factor in the region's literature, one must seek its effects not only in fictions wholly involved with motion pictures like Fitzgerald's *Last Tycoon* and Budd Schulberg's *What Makes Sammy Run?* but in those only marginally involved with the industry like Horace McCoy's *They Shoot Horses, Don't They?* or in fictions like those of Raymond Chandler for the most part unconcerned with motion pictures.

A careful look at such works makes it clear that there *is* an aesthetically significant Hollywood-Southland regionalism. (The term *Southland*, a journalistic geo-logism, is convenient shorthand for the sweep of coastal basins, ranges, and inland valleys that constitutes southern California.) Hollywood-Southland can be seen, simultaneously, as a literary region with its own identity, and as part of a broader California regionalism.[13] It is a region which begins to emerge in the 1920s, roughly coincident with Los Angeles's transformation from hick town to metropolis and, indeed, with the coming of age of the motion picture industry. Among influences upon its literature, it shares with the rest of California a geophysical immensity and an unparalleled variety of landscape; a societal newness and a lack of history save for a relatively recent frontier and agrarian past; and a magnetic appeal for seekers after fortune, fame or salvation. These shared characteristics are joined, in Hollywood-Southland, by a number of specifically local influences sufficient to justify its claim to separate regionality: a static and languorous subtropical climate; the rapid movement of events and people characteristic of the twentieth-century metropolis; a sprawling stucco and neon landscape set precariously in a land of drought, flood, and earthquake, its structures almost as tentative as Hollywood sets, and almost as changeable; the movie industry itself; several hundred miles of shoreline, and an omnipresent sea. It is a region whose century-and-a-quarter English-speaking past is rich with adventurous diarists, moralistic journalists, resident romantics, and imitative versifiers, but one which lagged behind northern California in giving rise to a serious literature. One of Hollywood-Southland's more obvious demographic characteristics is, in fact, its twentieth-century assumption of San Francisco's nineteenth-century role as far-western metropolis, a role which in the north helped to spawn Mark Twain and turn-of-the-century writers like Frank Norris and Jack London. Interestingly, with its emergence in the twentieth century, the Southland region has proved to be, unlike the earlier San Francisco, almost exclusively a prose fiction region.

The hyphenated rubric, Hollywood-Southland, seems the

most accurate to apply to this literary region, for although the aesthetic region is not confined to Hollywood, Hollywood and the motion picture industry do constitute its thematic and symbolic core. To the literary sensibility, Hollywood remains regional "ground zero." All else is suburb. Those characteristics of the Southland which inform its fiction, though spread throughout the region, are invariably more pronounced, more concentrated, and more intensely experienced the closer one moves toward its Hollywood epicenter.

The task before us — elucidation of both an hypothesis and a body of fiction — creates a problem of number. We need to look at sufficiently many works to establish any patterns of regional consistency that may appear, yet at few enough to allow, within space limitations, for a detailed look at each fiction. Eight works should suffice to provide that optimum breadth: James M. Cain's *The Postman Always Rings Twice* (1934), Horace McCoy's *They Shoot Horses, Don't They?* (1935), John O'Hara's *Hope of Heaven* (1938), Nathanael West's *The Day of the Locust* (1939), Raymond Chandler's *Farewell, My Lovely* (1940), Budd Schulberg's *What Makes Sammy Run?* (1941), Scott Fitzgerald's *Pat Hobby Stories* (1939 to 1941) and *The Last Tycoon* (1941). Their seven-year span is brief enough to minimize the passage of time as a variable. That those same seven years produced what remains the region's richest literary output is also no small factor in selecting this focus. Among the eight are fictions as deeply involved with the movie industry as Fitzgerald's *Tycoon* and Schulberg's *Sammy*, and as unconcerned with it as Chandler's *Farewell* and Cain's *Postman*. Apart from the region in which all are set and in which their authors wrote, they are unquestionably a mixed lot.

What then does applying our regional hypothesis to these fictions demonstrate? Among other things, it provides a number of heretofore unavailable insights into the works themselves. No less notably, though, there emerges a complex yet remarkably consistent pattern of effects which Hollywood-Southland seems to have upon its fictions, effects which *in toto* define the Holywood-Southland literary region. Themes, motifs, narrative techniques, attitudes, assumptions—all of which constitute the aesthetic heart of a piece of literature—can be seen recurring throughout these fictions, however various the works seem at first glance.

Dominating the fictions and unifying them is a single, overriding theme. It is a theme of *dissolution,* a generalized breaking down of the old, the traditional, the real, and the substantive—at times replaced by new, less substantive, less meaningful, even deadly substitutes, and at other times replaced by nothing. This all-pervasive coming apart manifests itself variously. Amongst characters, both major and minor, we see repeatedly a loss of innocence; innocence gives way, though, not to sophistication or wisdom but to cynicism, morbidity, or hollow jadedness. In a succession of characters, we also see a loss of motivation and direction; purpose becomes aimlessness, and motivation gives way to listlessness or a compulsive consumption of energy. Traditional values break down and are replaced by new, more superficial and self-serving ones. Personal dreams are shattered, sometimes even the capacity to dream; weary resignation fills the void. Lost too is any sense of belonging; in its place we see transience, impermanence, adriftness. The ability, even the will, to love is destroyed, and with it normal sexuality; callousness, isolation, and perversion fill the void. Quite often the characters' sense of worth and self-adequacy is dissipated. Personal identity falls into doubt. Normal sense perceptions fade or blur. The life of the spirit dwindles and dies. With disproportionate frequency in these fictions, life itself is destroyed.

Beyond the lives of individuals, human relationships in general break down, and with them the capacity for human communication; fear, envy, and distrust dominate. Language itself, man's primary means of social cohesion, becomes less reliable: its meanings are often broadened beyond recognition, diluted by cliché, reversed, or otherwise distorted or blurred. Traditional patterns of authority come apart; authority figures are at best ineffectual, at worst impotent or corrupt. Art and the aesthetic impulse fade in these narratives, replaced by a drive toward slickness and dollar profit. That nexus of myths, hopes, and aspirations known as the

Great American Dream figures heavily in these fictions—with Hollywood usually its objective epitome—and almost without exception we see the Dream wither and die. Dissolution is everywhere.

Tied to this dominant theme throughout the works is a network of reinforcive themes and motifs. Violence is endemic. Narrative action often undergoes kinetic speed-up. A pervasive two-dimensionality afflicts not only things but people. The distinction between reality and illusion is thrown into doubt. Façade, deception, and the playing of roles assume major importance. Incongruity abounds.

The prevailing narrative tone in Southland fiction—another virtual constant—is one of irony and cynicism. Its world view is consistently deterministic, with an authorial moralism never far beneath the surface. With the exception of Fitzgerald's *Last Tycoon*, each of the fictions seems more interested in moral abstraction or hell-bent action than character delineation or social portraiture.

Fundamental qualities of style and narrative technique in these works are also influenced by their involvement with region. Plot structures tend to be cinematic. Narration is consistently first-person and decidedly more sensorial than reflective; it is highly visual and unambiguous. Hyperbole is a recurrent narrative mode.

Beyond theme, motif, style, and tone, each of the fictions draws for aesthetic effect, upon a common store of regional items and idiosyncrasies. The fictions share many of the same insights into the region upon which they draw, and most of their attitudes about it. In short, these works—though they vary greatly in achievement and in their dependence upon place—possess an essential aesthetic affinity for each other. And that affinity is, for the most part, regional.

2

The Postman and the Marathon

Edmund Wilson notwithstanding, it seems clear that Horace McCoy's *They Shoot Horses, Don't They?* (1935) was not derived, consciously or otherwise, from James M. Cain's *The Postman Always Rings Twice* (1934). Though unpublished for some nineteen months after *Postman*, this first and better of McCoy's two Hollywood novels had been on paper in shorter form since mid-1932, and completed in first draft since late 1933. McCoy disliked Cain's work and resented being identified with it. However innocent, though, of paternity in this one case (and of quality in general), Cain's *Postman* remains his prototypical work, and the most influential of his long string of minor novels, nourishing not only the voguishly "tough" novels of the next twenty years but as central a twentieth-century work as Camus' *L'Étranger*. Conceived then by two Hollywood writers independently of one another at about the same time, both ultimately more important as influences than attainments (especially to French existentialists), both set in the Hollywood-Southland periphery and drawing little (at least not obviously) upon the motion picture industry, Cain's *Postman* and McCoy's *They Shoot Horses* give us excellent starting ground from which to explore an emergent literary region in southern California.

The dissolution motif which dominates the region's fiction is abundantly evident in both novels. Old realities, values, and aspirations, such as they are, collapse. Relationships between characters repeatedly break down amidst violence and shallow passion, and they rematerialize into new, less gratifying and more tenuous relationships—until the final destruction. In *Postman*, Nick Papadakis's marriage, happy at least from his own naïve standpoint, is quickly undone by Frank Chambers's chance arrival and seduction of Cora. One bloody episode, his bathroom "accident," costs Nick grievous injury and his wife's estrangement. After their tenuous reconciliation, a second such episode high above Malibu Canyon costs him his life. At this point, love's triangle seems to have resolved itself, brutally but resolutely. But as the love-killers seek new equilibrium living together—and Cain is not averse, amidst the blood and gore, to sentimentalizing this quest— new breakdowns occur. Frank's plan to escape the consequences of Nick's murder falls apart, along with his courage and equanimity, at the hands of a bullying district attorney who coerces him into saving his own skin and signing a criminal complaint against Cora. "I didn't want to do it," Frank later pleads to Cora. "I tried not to do it. But he beat me down. I cracked up, that's all." Saved only by the connivance of her attorney, Cora thereafter seeks self-redemption. Her attempts to improve Nick's roadside tavern, to build its patronage and *be* something, to reform Frank, to have his baby—all begin promisingly, then are shattered: by Frank's continuing wanderlust, by the threat of blackmail from her attorney's ex-aide, by revelation of Frank's infidelity, and finally by the fatal highway crash.

So too in McCoy's novel does life move inexorably downward toward destruction. Like Cora, Gloria Beatty is killed at the end; like Frank, Robert Syverten is delivered to the executioner. The lives of almost three hundred young people are reduced to the meaningless and depraved circularity of a marathon dance. Before dying, both Robert and Gloria see their fondest dreams fade. Like Cora, who had quickly sunk from celebrity to hashslinger, Gloria had come to Hollywood to be in pictures. Unlike Cora, Gloria is unable to muster a substitute dream. Robert's dreams also decline, from at first an ambition to work "for Von Sternberg, or Mamoulian or Boleslawsky . . . learning about composition and tempo and angles," to a hope to go to work for a beer company after the marathon, then, with his sentence of death, to no hope at all.

Even Robert's subconscious dramatizes this fall: during one of his agonizingly brief ten-minute sleeps at the marathon, he dreams he is "the most important picture director in the world" plunging from the deck of a luxury liner into shark-infested waters below. Minor characters in the novel, such as Lillian Bacon, also bespeak this theme of shattered dreams. After she and her partner, Pedro Ortega, win one of the marathon's early sponsors, she sighs, "As long as it couldn't be Metro-Goldwyn-Mayer it might as well be a garage."

The death of dreams and dreamers has, in fact, been a theme pervading California narratives since the "bust" days of the Gold Rush. One of California's earliest imaginative chroniclers, Alonzo Delano, describes his encounter with a ragged effigy "among the diggings." Pinned to the dummy's chest was an epitaph:

> Californians! O! Californians! look at me. Once as fat and saucy as a privateersman; but now—look ye—a miserable skeleton. In a word, a used man. Never mind, I can sing away notwithstanding:

> > O, Californy! This is the land for me,
> >   A pick and shovel, and lots of bones,
> > Who would not come, the sight to see?
> >   The golden land of dross and stones!
> > O, Susannah! don't you cry for me,
> >   I'm *living dead* in Californ—ee! [1]

In both Cain and McCoy, traditional ethical values go the way of dreams, corrupted by crassness and cheapness at every turn. Cora is saved from execution not by anyone's compassion or commitment to truth, but because her lawyer Katz is slicker and more unscrupulous than District Attorney Sackett. Most important for Katz is his hundred-dollar bet with Sackett on the outcome of the trial. Sackett, on the other hand, simply needs someone, anyone, to prosecute. Cora's life is only a pawn in their game of chance. Cain hints rather crudely at the death of truth by basing most of Sackett's prosecution upon the erroneous eye-witness testimony of a Mr. Wright. Clearly, Wright is wrong. Katz can say to Cora right after the verdict that frees her (and before magnanimously waiving his fee): "Not so fast. There's one other little thing. That ten thousand dollars [insurance money] you get for knocking off the Greek."

The same motif of corrupted values pervades *They Shoot Horses*. It's not how you play the game, but winning that counts. You succeed, or you're a bum. "I'm jealous of anybody who's a success," Gloria says to Robert, "aren't you?" "Certainly not," he answers, to which she replies, "You're a fool." Chivalry, too, is dead. When Gloria persists in urging abortion on Ruby Bates, Ruby's husband slugs her. Nobleness, which flickers hopefully as Robert intercedes, fades just as quickly when he jerks his knee up between his adversary's legs. As Robert says, "It was the only chance I had." When another contestant, Mattie Barnes, faints with menstrual fatigue, her partner slaps her sharply and complains to the other dancers about *his* hard luck with marathon partners. The marathon's promoter, Socks Donald, is a tough-talking catalog of broken values. Enraged over a contestant's arrest on the dance floor as an escaped murderer, Socks abjures when resultant publicity sends attendance soaring. Later, he implores Robert and Gloria to be married during the marathon. "You can get divorced if you want to," Socks argues. "It don't have to be permanent. It's just a showmanship angle." (It turns out that the pregnant Ruby and her husband James had themselves been married during an Oklahoma marathon.) When another couple, Vee Lovell and Mary Hawley, consent to the plan, emcee Rocky Gravo heralds the event as "high-class entertainment." As a prize for faithful attendance at the marathon, the management bestows upon Mrs. Layden the epitome of worthlessness—a season's pass to more marathon dancing.

One value in particular—the aesthetic—undergoes corruption in *They Shoot Horses*, as it does throughout Southland fiction. Art after art goes out, and all is cash, a naked impulse toward slickness and dollar profit. Scarcely a commentator on Hollywood has neglected the theme. By the thirties, the film industry—where Cain and McCoy both worked—had assumed first rank in the demonology of serious writers. It was the capitol of anti-art, the home of the Big Sell-Out, a place where writers were paid very well to build, preserve, and enhance illusions—but never examine them. (This two-edged theme was later to receive its most incisive treatment in Evelyn Waugh's *The Loved One*, 1948, a mordant satire in which Southland morticians become the artists, creating a new and lucrative art form out of the decaying flesh of their clientele.) McCoy's marathon itself is sustained perversion of an art form. Its dancers seem willing to tolerate every degradation to stay in the running for the thousand-dollar prize.

Another of the Southland's most recurrent motifs of dissolution is evident in both novels: that of lost roots, the sense of transience and aimless drifting which results when one is cut off from his past. Like the perished dream, the theme of rootlessness has been central to California writing since the Gold Rush, and in large measure nourishes the theme of broken values. Frank Chambers is a drifter who never loses the impulse to drift. Born in "Frisco" (a verbal corruption which home-loving San Franciscans deplore), his immediate past consists of three weeks in the shabby border city of Tia Juana. Sackett later establishes that Frank has bummed in Kansas City, New York, New Orleans, Chicago, and been in jail in Tucson, Salt Lake City, San Diego, Wichita, Oakland, Los Angeles. Cora herself is a displaced midwesterner, and Nick a foreigner. Even Frank's "homecoming" —his return to the roadside beanery after Nick finds him in Glendale—is, as Frank puts it, "the worst flop of a homecoming you ever saw in your life." Both Robert and Gloria, like Cain's trio, come from somewhere else. Both search aimlessly in Hollywood for a sense of belonging, their rootlessness underscored by the marathon's role as their only source of bed and board.

One manifestation of this rootlessness repeatedly played upon by Southland writers is a loss of, or a confusion over, personal identity. If Natty Bumppo can be said to have established rapport with the land by naming its flora and fauna, Hollywood writers (not alone among moderns, but virtually *en bloc*) have implied societal disassociation by, in a sense, *un*naming things—by throwing identity into doubt. Frank's affair with the lady animal trainer begins with an explicit question of identity:

> "So your name is Madge Allen, hey?"
> "Well, it's really Kramer, but I took my own name again after my husband died."
> "Well listen, Madge Allen, or Kramer, or whatever you want to call it, I've got a little proposition to make you." [2]

Cora's identity is called into question early in the novel; to Frank she looks "a little bit Mex." "My name was Smith before I was married," she snarls. "That doesn't sound much like a Mex, does it?" Indeed it doesn't. In her American context, Cora's maiden name, Smith, bestows as much anonymity as a name possibly can. Later, when drawn to him, she fears that Frank will "begin calling her Mrs. Papadakis." Nick's identity too is symbolically torn away—before literally deprived him—when a hot desert wind blows down his sign. The plot itself turns on a question of confused identity, that of the court stenographer who takes Cora's confession. Though less developed in *They Shoot Horses*, the identity theme is suggested there too with the arrest of Giuseppe Lodi, the convicted murderer, dancing in the marathon under an alias.[3]

Also victim to the generalized dissolution which pervades both novels is any semblance of genuine love. Even Nick's devotion to Cora is marred by his contempt for womanhood. Frank's love for her—or the animal sexuality that passes for it—is, by his own admission, tarnished by fear; and "when you get fear in it," he tells her, "it's not love anymore. It's hate." The moment Cora is out of sight, Frank puts the make on Madge Allen. Madge's resumption of her maiden name after her husband's death further suggests the breakdown and defilement of love in the world inhabited by Cain's characters. The same loss of capacity to love is suggested by McCoy in giving Gloria "heart trouble," heart trouble, though, which Robert "knew [the doctor] could never locate . . . with a stethoscope."

Not only love, but normal sexuality breaks down—another theme at the center or edges of virtually all Southland fiction.

At the drop of a hormone, Frank and Cora hurl themselves lustfully at one another, teeth bared and knuckles whitened, in what seems at first an unsubtle parody of sadomasochistic frenzy. In the apparent intimacy of their marathon partnership, Gloria can tell Robert, "I've about made up my mind that I've been letting the wrong sex try to make me." Upon arriving at the dance hall, the first things they see are "two male and female nurses"—the ambiguity is flagrant.

A loss of even the most minimal human compassion, much less love, pervades both novels. When compassion does appear, it is fleeting. And it is the kind of compassion fatal to its object. Rushing Cora to the hospital as she miscarries, Frank crashes and kills her. Sympathetic with Gloria in her deep depression, Robert fires a bullet into her head. Human relationships are fouled. Ruby and James, with whom Gloria and Robert first argue, then brawl, are called by Robert, "our best friends in the dance." The apparently maternal affection of Mrs. Layden for the two becomes a bid by the old lady to "keep" Robert when the marathon ends. Robert and Gloria spend thirty-seven days and nights in each other's arms, yet never really come to be friendly, or even know one another.

As a convenient correlative for this general breakdown of human ties, Cain, like other California writers, exploits the virulent anti-Mexican prejudice regionally at hand. (Hardly a nineteenth-century California narrative is without its inferior Mexican or Oriental, an exuberant ethnocentrism one critic has called California's "Anglo-vitamin vigor." [4]) As *Postman* opens, Frank arrives at the Twin Oaks up from slumming in Tia Juana. Cora fears that Frank will think her a "Mex." Even so congenial a character as Madge Allen condescends toward Mexican virtuousness: "That's one thing about a Mexican," she tells Frank. "He's slow but he's honest." Ethnocentrically impartial, Frank and Cora both despise Nick's "black kinky hair" and his Greek "greasiness." There is also, in the shyster Katz (besides his obvious homonymic relationship to the novel's numerous cats) clear anti-Semitic innuendo. Like *Postman*, *They Shoot Horses* has its own (though fewer) intimations of bigotry. Completely in character, Socks Donald can call Giuseppe Lodi a "dirty wop son of a bitch." But when Mrs. Higby from the Mother's League also slurs his Italianness, we sense how inveterate this bigotry really is.

Another regionally recurrent correlative for the coming apart of human relationships—and a predictable one when seen as a product of literary sensibilities—is a breakdown in man's primary means of communication, his language. Though not elaborately developed by either Cain or McCoy, the phenomenon is evident in *They Shoot Horses,* largely in the person of Rocky Gravo whose incessant ballyhoo alternately stretches language beyond referential recognition or reduces it to pitiful cliché. Gloria, too, speaks in hand-me-down phrases. "I'm tired of living and I'm afraid of dying," she tells Robert in all seriousness. Overhearing her, James Bates cracks "that's a swell idea for a song."

One of the most interesting manifestations of breakdown in Southland fiction—and another frontier vestige—is its consistently disparaging portrayal of formal authority. Authority is pictured as either impotent, unduly harsh, or corrupt. The policeman who happens upon Frank and Cora's first murder attempt is satisfied that the peculiar circumstances he encounters—Frank's standing nervously beneath the second-story window with the lights short-circuited—are the fault of a ladder-climbing cat's having stepped into a fuse box. The district attorney is little more than a crude inquisitor, indifferent as to whom he prosecutes, unconcerned that his evidence is reliable, and not even sufficiently clever to outmaneuver the sleazy Katz. Katz, in turn, makes a mockery of the law by arranging to defend both Frank and Cora. The legal process itself, which permits the sham, is but an amoral chess game. Frank is referred to Katz in the first place by a policeman—for a cut of the action. At McCoy's marathon, the "judge" counting laps in the "derby" seems indeed to have wrongly disqualified Jere Flint and his partner; it is, as Jere claims, "a goddam frame up. . . . If Vee and Mary [who had seemed the losers] had been eliminated you wouldn't have a wedding tomorrow—" The City Council, in spite of ugly publicity and Mothers' League protests, seems unable to close down the marathon; it closes on its own after the double slaying. The court itself is decidedly unbeneficent: Robert pleads that it has ignored the mitigating circumstances surrounding Gloria's death, and as the narrative unfolds we come to believe him. With its sentence of death, the court serves justice not only blindly, but brutally.

In both novels, innocence is damned. It gives way, in Gloria's case, before the novel opens, not to wisdom or sophistication but to a hollow jadedness. For Nick and for Robert, innocence gives way to death. There is also, throughout the region's fiction and apparent in both novels, a motif of youthful energy and vital life force being turned to corrupt or meaningless ends. It pervades McCoy's, with all his youthful contestants expending great stores of vitality in the grotesque circularity of the marathon dance. Lost, too, is any sense of self-worth. Bereft of it herself, Gloria is compelled to deprive others of their own sense of adequacy and well-being. And she succeeds. During derby preparations, she tells Robert snidely that jockstraps "come in three sizes: small, medium, and large. You take a small." Before shooting her, Robert tells Gloria

> you ought to change your attitude. On the level. It affects everybody you come in contact with. Take me, for example. Before I met you I didn't see how I could miss succeeding. I never even thought of failing. And now—[5]

The value of life itself is severely diminished in *They Shoot Horses*. Early in the narrative, Robert likens the marathon to a bullfight, its contestants the fated bulls. When asked at the end by the arresting officers, "Why did you kill her?" he can reply, "They shoot horses, don't they?" As the patrol car takes him away, sirens—which during the dance had been a symbol of life, awakening the dancers after each ten-minute break—now designate death, both Gloria's and Robert's. In a sense, those sirens help to obliterate the distinction between life and death. During the narrative both Gloria and Robert express a death wish, Gloria incessantly, Robert more obliquely as he sneaks a longing look at an archetypal ocean sunset through the dance hall door, and later tells us,

"I've had enough ocean to last me the rest of my life."

It should be noted amongst the novel's details that the beer company which finally sponsors Robert and Gloria in the dance, and the one on which Robert pins his hopes for a future, is named *Jonathan*—with its unmistakable implications of the hope and energy of a younger America. That all-embracing set of values that breaks down before our eyes—in McCoy, in Cain, and in most Southland fiction—is nothing less than the Great American Dream. Gloria Beatty's name represents its glory beaten. Hardly coincidental are the marathon's end, and Gloria's death, at the turn of the thirty-eighth day, the span of time on America's Christian calendar between Ash Wednesday and Good Friday, forty days minus two; resurrection is not a factor. In *Postman,* the Dream's demise, as David Madden has observed, takes the shape of a fatal collision between two major elements of the American myth.[6] Frank is a frontier type caught in the throes of the Great Depression: unreflective, impulsive, violent, a low-level con man, a believer in the attainability of anything so long as one is bold enough to grab for it, and addicted, when complications arise, to moving on. His past reads like a jumbled American gazetteer. Cora is middle-American, a small-town Iowan Miss Smith who ventures out in search of the romantic grail, Hollywood stardom. Though it eludes her, she can still fall back upon inbred yearnings for respectability, and profit. In their criminal affair, we see these two central facets of the American character—unrestrained mobility and respectable sedentariness—and two views of the American landscape—the open road and the mortgaged house—collide, and in colliding, destroyed.

Beyond the dominant dissolution motif, there appear in both novels a number of reinforcive motifs which recur throughout Southland fiction. Among the most pervasive is violence, actual and threatened. Since its nineteenth-century beginnings, Southland narrative has leaned heavily upon the motif, a seemingly compulsive and often gratuitous violence, a normative violence. Indicative is an early John Phoenix "poem" called "Sandy-Ago" in which the night's most common sound is "the pleasant screak of the victim/Whose

been shot prehaps in his gizzard." [7] In *Postman*, Nick dies
violently, Cora dies violently, and Frank is about to die violently as the narrative ends. Frank and Cora's love, such as
it is, is a violent animal lusting. Frank sinks his teeth into
Cora's lips, drives his fist into her leg, and "rips" her at her
own moaning behest in scene after scene of erotic mayhem.
It is significant that after his brief fling, Frank forsakes the
animal *tamer*, Madge, to return to Cora, the "hell cat." In
They Shoot Horses, James smacks Gloria, Robert brawls
with James, Pedro slugs Lillian and knifes Rocky Gravo,
Socks blackjacks Pedro, Jere punches the floor judge, Mrs.
Layden and an unnamed man are shot to death, and finally
Robert kills Gloria. Throughout, the dance floor is rife with
latent hostility. It is a strength of McCoy's novel that its
violence is rendered with more restraint and matter-of-fact-
ness—and is thus more chilling—than the snarling revelry of
Cain's *Postman*.

Another motif shared by the novels is the illusion of a
speed-up in time. Complementing the losses of value and
substance is a more rapid pace of action, a sense of the narrative projector's running at higher speed. Things happen
faster. They begin more quickly and are resolved more
quickly. It takes but two weeks for Cora to go from celebrity
to hash house, extraordinary speed even for Hollywood. Frank
and Cora are in bed by the end of their second brief chat.
Cora's trial for murder is over in less than twenty-four hours.
Frank no sooner learns Madge Allen's name than he proposi-
tions her. The relationship between Robert and Gloria develops no less quickly. They meet accidentally on Melrose
Avenue, "and when we got to Western," says Robert, "I knew
she was Gloria Beatty, an extra who wasn't doing well either,
and she knew a little about me. I liked her very much." It
was that quick. Every meal, every sleep, every contact with
life (save with one's partner) is forced into maddeningly
brief ten-minute interludes between dances. Every dance
period ends with a sprint. Every night the "derby" imposes
its frenetic pace upon the contestants. Certainly no factor
in McCoy's novel contributes more to this sense of accelerated time than its narrative perspective, an interior mono-

logue elapsing entirely within the moment of Robert's sentencing.

Closely tied to this kinetic speed-up—and an obvious concomitant to the regional breakdown in values—is a motif of two-dimensionality, a flat insubstantiality afflicting both character and object. Perhaps, as Frederick Bracher speculates, a powerful topography like the Southland's tends to minimize, in the eye of the artist, the significance of the man-made, and of man himself, encouraging this flatness.[8] Like images flashing rapidly across a screen, the characters of both novels, and in most of the region's fictions, are bare stereotypes sketched fleetingly in a few broad strokes. In *Postman* we have the vicious drifter (Frank), the tough but passionate harlot (Cora), the warm-hearted naïf (Nick), the hard-nosed prosecutor (Sackett), the shyster lawyer (Katz), the easy lay (Madge)—a dramatis personae referred to by Stanley Hyman as Cain's "picturesque cardboard characters." The tag names Cain gives them—Frank (indeed he is), Cora (the rudimentary creature, the core)—do nothing to dispel this sense of flatness. McCoy's people, too, are stereotypes. Gloria is jaded, hard-bitten from the start, a foul-mouthed graduate of the school of hard knocks, old before her time, with traces of compassion flickering briefly but smothered by a calloused exterior. Robert, at the start, is wide-eyed and hopeful, a gullible outsider adrift in hell and about to go under. Significantly, both Robert and Gloria, as McCoy originally conceived them in the story's shorter version, were more rounded and complex, more like "real" people. But as the conception of his Hollywood *danse macabre* grew more important, McCoy forced himself to scale the pair down, to redraw them in bolder, flatter strokes. His minor characters—Rocky, Socks, the various couples—are also bare representations of type. Gloria and Robert, even more clearly than Cora and Nick, are a pair of two-dimensional opposites common to Southland fiction: the jaded initiate and the vulnerable naïf.

Motifs of deceit, deception, and façade also mark both novels (though less elaborately than elsewhere in the Southland corpus). Cora cheats on Nick, Frank cheats on Cora, and Frank and Cora cheat the executioner—temporarily.

Their deception fools Nick fatally, and in collusion with Katz they almost fool society by escaping conviction. In *They Shoot Horses*, Rosemary Loftus cheats on her partner and lures Robert under the canvas, a liaison which fails only because Gloria, more practiced at the game, has already snuck away from Robert to lust beneath the same canvas with Rocky Gravo. Lillian Bacon cheats on Pedro beneath the platform. Even old Mrs. Layden, after first befriending Gloria, slanders her behind her back. Throughout the narrative, Socks, his assistant Rollo Peters, and Rocky all turn their energies toward making the marathon, and the incidents which befall it, seem other than what they are. "Look at these kids," Rocky gloats to the crowd as the couples shuffle around the floor, "they are as fresh as a daisy. . . . These kids are fed seven times a day. . . . they are in the best of physical condition." After Rocky is knifed by Pedro, stirring the crowd, Rollo assures them it is merely the rehearsal of a novelty act.

The most pervasive of the many motifs which unify Southland fiction is the juxtaposition of illusion and reality, and the consequent confusion between them. Certainly the regional omnipresence of the movie industry encourages this motif, as does the industry's more direct influence on those who write its scenarios and thereafter turn to fiction. But it is a motif fostered by other and broader influences within the region, a region whose mountains are often snowcapped in summer, whose rivers and lakes are usually dry, whose arid landscape is often devastated by flood, whose climate alters dramatically within very short distances, whose rural periphery is a desert turned into soil of unsurpassed fertility. And Hollywood in the thirties is, as S. J. Perelman recalls, still something of a boomtown, making "news of breadlines and starvation unreal." [9] Twice early in *They Shoot Horses*, Robert's recollections slip smoothly out of reality into illusion. Rebuffed at the studio door by an apprentice director, Robert imagines himself riding away in a Rolls-Royce "having people point me out as the greatest director in the world." Then he meets Gloria, they walk to a park, and reality once more fades into illusion:

It was a fine place to sit. . . . but it was very dark and very quiet and filled with dense shrubbery. All around it palm trees grew up, fifty, sixty feet tall, suddenly tufted at the top. Once you entered the park you had the illusion of security. I often imagined they were sentries wearing grotesque helmets: my own private sentries, standing guard over my private island.

When they get to the dance hall, among the first things they see is "a house doctor . . . [who] didn't look like a doctor at all." Though underplayed by Cain (whose first glimpse of Los Angeles took in a man rowing around under some palm trees during a rainstorm), the clash between reality and illusion does surface at several points in *Postman*: most clearly as Frank stands beside the wreckage of Nick's car in the ravine, his voice sounding "queer, like it was coming out of a tin phonograph."

This blurring of reality and illusion is reinforced by frequent incongruity. The incongruous image or circumstance becomes a standard technique in Southland fiction. Moments after bludgeoning Nick and hurling him down the embankment, Frank and Cora flout consequence and fornicate alongside his bloody corpse. The deadly serious matter of Giuseppe's recapture at the marathon is made possible by his picture's appearing in a frivolous detective monthly. The tranquillity of the park is guarded over by grotesques. Rocky repeatedly bids the music to begin ("Give," he commands) and turns up the volume on the radio. *Non sequiturs*, like the frequent contention that "these kids love [the marathon]. Every one of them has gained weight . . ." only heighten the effect.

In tone as in theme, the region's fiction unifies with remarkable consistency. Its voice is invariably ironic, its outlook deterministic, and its posture usually that of the finger-wagging moralist. Albert Van Nostrand goes so far as to call irony *Postman's raison d'être*. "The novel has no theme, no attitude toward its subject," he argues. "It simply tells how the murderers ironically escaped until they were ironically punished." [10] Certainly the moral that, according to Cain, informs all his fiction—the terrifying outcome of the wish that comes true—is fundamentally ironic.[11] Most of *Postman*'s action takes place at Nick's "roadside sandwich joint," the Twin Oaks Tavern, whose connotations of stability and union are a blatant mockery of the two unstable partnerships it shelters. After the murder, Frank and Cora's savior-apparent comes to them in the weasely form of Katz, "a little guy, about forty years old, with a leathery face and a black moustache," and a half-burned cigarette hanging out the side of his mouth. The punishment for killing which they escape in court—in spite of Sackett and their own confessions—overtakes them accidentally at the culvert wall in the midst of their only life-saving gesture of the story. Frank is finally executed for a crime that never happened (his "murder" of Cora) while the real murder, Nick's, goes legally unpunished. Though Frank himself lacks a sense of the ironies which enmesh him, Cora does not. She accepts the baby puma from Madge, then laughs wildly at Frank: "And the cat came back! It stepped on the fuse box and got killed, but here it is back! Ha, ha, ha, ha, ha, ha, ha! Ain't that funny, how unlucky cats are for you?"

Of McCoy's many ironies perhaps the most striking is his novel's last: that a man so victimized by circumstances as Robert is asked—and consents—to play God in destroying Gloria. And it is irony impelled, in McCoy as in most of his Hollywood contemporaries, by moral revulsion over his Southland subject. His widow recalls how profoundly shaken he was by the "bestiality" of dance marathons. Within the marathon hall certain props are placed solely for ironic effect —like the Palm Garden with its suggestions of a tranquil oasis mocking its reality as the site of double murder. The nightly derby is an ironic perversion of most such races: here there is no prize for winning, only elimination for the losers. Robert's attempt to explain killing Gloria as an act of compassion is cut short by the judge's intoning, "is there any legal cause why sentence should not now be pronounced?" His lawyer's reiterated plea that compassion mitigate the penalty is interrupted by the judge's gavel and verdict, "There being no legal cause. . . ." Much of the novel's irony is imagistic, like the "big triangle of sunshine" Robert describes coming through the window above the bar in the Palm Garden:

> It only lasted about ten minutes but during those ten minutes I moved slowly about in it . . . letting it cover me completely. It was the first time I had ever appreciated the sun. . . .
>
> I watched the triangle on the floor get smaller and smaller. Finally it closed altogether and started up my legs. It crawled up my body like a living thing. When it got to my chin I stood on my toes to keep my head in it as long as possible. I did not close my eyes. I kept them wide open, looking straight into the sun. It did not blind me at all. In a moment it was gone.

Robert has his "moment in the sun"; it is both real and a tantalizing illusion. The light crawls seductively up his body while at the same time fading. Then it rises up beyond him out of reach. Ironic too is the imagery employed to render Mrs. Layden's death. She is shot while the Reverend Oscar Gilder recites the 23rd Psalm, and her corpse punctuates the prayer with its own "cup runneth over": her "head slowly turned sidewise and a little pool of blood that had collected in the crater of her eye spilled out on the floor."

The determinism implicit in Cora's death and Frank's execution is brought even closer to the surface by McCoy. The dancers move day and night to the music's beat and to the commands and sirens of the management. Occasionally one of them lashes out, and pays a heavy price. Circumstances are beyond the contestants' control. When the rules of the inhumanly grueling derby are spelled out to them, "None of the contestants had anything to say." Of little significance to the plot itself, Gloria's sordid upbringing in Texas is detailed to suggest the lasting effects of early environment. Her one confrontation with orthodox morality, the Mothers' League, leaves her "shaking and twitching with emotion, as if she had completely lost control of *the upper half* of her body" [italics mine]. That upper half, her head and her heart, may be jarred by the encounter, but presumably she never loses control of the lower half, the legs and genitals she survives by. If the bold and immense geophysiognomy of California *are* reductive of man, as Bracher speculates, then certainly the prevailing determinism of its fiction (evident in Norris, London, Jeffers, Steinbeck, and others, as well as in Hollywood writers) owes heavily, like the Southland's two-dimensional motif, to regional landscape.

As though to compensate for this insignificance and to overcome the numbed perceptions of a languorous milieu, Southland narrators tend frequently toward hyperbole, the figurative shout. Situations are overstated, characters exaggerated, phenomena overplayed. At times reality itself is made to seem hyperreal. Cain's narrator, Frank, insensitive to even the broadest of ironies, does see his world hyperbolically. His attraction to Cora is so immediate and overwhelming that he actually smells her sensuality and vomits for want of her. His violence, both the sensual and the murderous, assumes hyperbolic proportions. In a way, the whole narrative, up to the point of Nick's murder, is hyperbolic. It seems a parody, an exaggerated overdramatization of pulp fiction cliché: love at first sight, a masochistic heroine, extraordinary coincidence. Most of Cain's imagery—like Frank and Cora's corpse-side indulgence—is shaped by this impulse toward overstatement. Though less frequently than Cain, McCoy also depends upon the imagery of excess, with Gloria bearing much of the burden. She is preeminently a creature of excess. Her dislikes are excessive, and her depressions are excessive. Mrs. Layden sees that Gloria "hates everything and everybody." Robert tells us that she is "too blonde, too small and [looks] too old." Her most routine activity, a coffee break between dances, sees her taking four lumps of sugar "and lots of cream."

Other discernible similarities in narrative technique lend regional unity to the fictions. The first-person voice of both novels reflects the region's tendency toward participant narrators—perhaps to better establish credibility for the frequently incredible, or to excuse the lack of it. By denying us omniscience, the first-person voice also tacitly denies any substance that omniscience might probe. Characteristically,

Postman's narrative, conceived by Cain in the third person but switched in later drafts to the first-person voice of Frank Chambers, is rapidly paced, simply structured, and highly imagistic, appealing to the full spectrum of human senses. Frank is first attracted by the smell of night air at the Twin Oaks, then by the smell of Cora. He tastes her blood in their first embrace. He is sensitive to sounds, like the gurgling of a wine bottle next to Nick's dead body (sacramentally spilling his blood), and to tactile impressions like the crush of Nick's head beneath the wrench and the cool pressure of sea water as he dives in the surf near the novel's end. Both the influence of Hemingway (though Cain denies it) and Cain's own screenwriter's perspective encourage his fictional dependence upon terse, clipped dialogue to carry much of the novel's action. The scenarist in Cain is also betrayed in *Postman*'s neatly sequential narrative drawn upon a flashback. From one fellow screenwriter in particular, Vincent Lawrence (to whom *Postman* is dedicated), Cain learned to subordinate the search for "truth" in his writing to calculated technique. Van Nostrand observes that *Postman*, later made into a successful motion picture, reads like a movie continuity—which only echoes William Plomer's earlier judgment that the novel's effectiveness (such as it is) is "more like that of a film than of literature." [12] "In all its formal aspects," says Van Nostrand, the 30,000-word novel "was a scenario the moment it was published." [13]

McCoy's novel, also made into a successful motion picture, proceeds rapidly, like *Postman*, on the episodic recollections of a doomed first-person narrator. Like Frank's, much of Robert's narrative is rendered in terse, colloquial dialogue at times intended primarily to shock ("The cheese is beginning to bind," Gloria tells him). More loosely joined than *Postman*'s, the novel's brief episodes are, in effect, a series of tableaux projected against the unifying backdrop of an endurance contest. As such, the narrative demands—and gets from McCoy—a perceptual vividness quite in keeping with that of most Southland fiction. Robert's sensory equipment is fully at work bringing our own senses into play. In minute detail, he recalls the expression on Gloria's face at the bullet's impact. In the courtroom, his ears are attuned past the judge's intonement to a patchwork of incidental noises outside; he hears the judge "with his body." Throughout the dance, Robert feels the thrashing of waves upon the pilings beneath the dance hall pier. A kind of hyperbole is at work here too, intensifying the sensation of those waves, "surging through the balls of [Robert's] feet, as if they had been stethoscopes." Intensified too, by the simple expedient of increasingly larger and bolder type, is Robert's death sentence as we hear it uttered phrase by phrase between each scene.

Generally speaking, the aesthetic dependence of *Postman* upon region is slight, though hardly negligible. It is the region's mountainous periphery where Frank and Cora carry out their successful treachery against Nick. In California writing since its beginnings, the magnificent but harsh remoteness of cliff and mountain has served as a frequent setting for man's victimization at the hands of man or nature —as a reinforcive backdrop for acts both spectacular and cruel. Nick's last glance over the Malibu terrain is indeed, as Frank tells us, a "look out on those bad lands." The torrid Santa Ana winds that seasonally blast through mountain passes at up to a hundred miles an hour, are used symbolically to blow down Nick's sign, prefiguring the wayward passion soon to destroy him. The contrasting results of Frank's poolhall hustling in small-town San Bernardino and urban Glendale serve in small part to characterize him as a predestined loser once the stakes get high. Hinted at in Cora is the conventional Hollywood image of the beautiful but down-and-out heroine about to be found and won by her gallant hero— against which image Cain ironically contrasts and vivifies her. This near-starlet slinging hash in California "really wasn't any raving beauty," but one whose sulking lips her very unromantic hero wants "to mash . . . in for her." W. M. Frohock suggests that the whole Southland milieu plays an ongoing connotative role in the novel, a point pertinent beyond *Postman* to each of the fictions we will examine. "Somehow the phoniness of *The Postman* was less phony," says Frohock, "because the action was set in and around a hamburger joint in a part of California which had magnified the tawdriness of such places until the neon light and the false front created what was almost a special cosmos." [14]

Upon the particulars of that same Southland cosmos, McCoy's novel draws more richly than *Postman*. Most notably upon the surf, the meeting line of land and ocean. Its ebb and flow, ever perceptible to Robert, suggest not only the life-force waning in him and in Gloria, but a wider and incessant precariousness as it churns against the marathon's understructure. Throughout, the pier is "rising and falling and groaning and creaking with the movements of the water." And not just any oceanfront will do, for this, the California surf, is the end of the line for westward-moving American civilization and its manifest destiny. With a subtlety unmatched by Cain, McCoy reimplies the theme by playing symbolically on Hollywood street names. Robert meets Gloria after she misses her bus, and they "walk on down to Western." "When we got to Western," Robert tells us, "I knew she was Gloria Beatty. . . ." Later, when Robert glances out the dance hall door, the sun sinks into the ocean at "the end of the world." Sky and ocean at dusk forge an ominous, terminal redness to which Robert repeatedly alludes. When the marathon is canceled, Robert and Gloria exit into the damp, chill evening air and see the lights of Malibu—"where all the movie stars live"—flickering far down the shore northwest of them angling out and away from them. The success they both dreamed of is, in a matter of speaking, in sight, but receding out of reach, mockingly. With a smile on her face, Gloria (and all she represents) goes to her death, unresisting, "in that black night at the edge of the Pacific."

The outlook of McCoy's little novel upon place—certainly another measure of its regionality and one absent for the most part in *Postman*—is unequivocal. His harsh portrayal of "showmanship" at its crassest is intended—like his other Hollywood novel, *I Should Have Stayed Home* (1938)—to expose the dank underside of a superficially enchanting milieu. The marathon phenomenon was not limited to California but it did flourish there; and it epitomized for McCoy the sleazy life-style of Hollywood being played out against a spiritually anesthetizing backdrop. As the music drones on in the hall, we see life about to be born and life snuffed out; we see marriage, fraud, copulation, self-righteous reform (of a kind which flourished in the Southland in the thirties); we see a variety of personal crises and revelations, and at times even tender-heartedness—all of it as the isolated, Sisyphus-like society of dancers shuffles on.

In spite of Edmund Wilson's preference for Cain,[15] *They Shoot Horses* is better fiction than *Postman*. One critic puts it among the most original works of contemporary American fiction.[16] McCoy's characters do lack the fullness and credibility of motive Wilson feels they lack, but Cain's novel suffers as much in these respects, and with less justification. Though intentionally underdrawn, McCoy's protagonist-narrator Robert Syverten possesses a tonal and intellectual consistency Frank Chambers lacks. *They Shoot Horses* is also infused with subtleties wholly lacking in *Postman*. It is conceptually more unified and imaginatively far richer a novel. McCoy's central metaphor, the marathon on the pier, is sufficiently engrossing to overcome the novel's occasional narrative contrivance and stiltedness of dialogue (inadequacies that do become painfully obvious in *I Should Have Stayed Home*, which lacks so strong a governing image).

For all its vitality, Cain's *Postman* remains a forced, structurally imperfect, and meretricious novel, even by the minimal standards its defenders invoke. The heavy-handedness of its irony, hyperbole, and symbolism are unredeemed by any inventive turn or authorial insight. It panders shamelessly to subliterary taste. Frank's occasional bursts of piety—

> I kissed her. Her eyes were shining up at me like two blue stars. It was like being in church. . . .

> We lay there face to face, and held hands under water. I looked up at the sky. It was all you could see. I thought about God

—and his spiritual cleansing in the surf (decidedly imitative of Jake Barnes's at San Sebastian), test the credibility of even the least demanding reader. The story is melodramatic and far too dependent upon contrived coincidence and surprising twist. These are traits we are ready to accept—even appreciate—as parody, which is what the novel seems to be (in Wilson's words a "Devil's parody of the movies") until the tone shifts at Nick's murder and Cain seems to ask us to take his characters and their plight seriously thereafter. This apparently inadvertent tonal shift is the most serious of *Postman*'s many flaws. The novel's culminating irony, the fatal crash, is a *diabolus ex machina* of major proportions. The novel's brevity hardly tolerates the number of episodes it is asked to carry. And Frank is more a bare-chested comic-book swain than a credible reporter for the whole affair.

Though artistry and regionality are independent qualities, McCoy's novel is not only the better but the more regional of the two. It gives fuller expression to the dominant theme of dissolution, and generates a broader spectrum of the motifs that—as subsequent chapters should bear out—are tied to the region. It also draws more heavily upon specific regional items (though as we will see later on less so than fiction can), and it more successfully integrates those items into its narrative fabric. Taken together, however, both novels are edifying from our special standpoint. They clearly establish the ties between place and fiction that define the Hollywood-Southland region.

3

A Hopeless Southland Allegory

From our hypothesis on the relationship of region to literature, one gets as much mileage as he can reasonably expect
if the work before him receives some measure of illumination
beyond that afforded by other approaches. In the case, however, of John O'Hara's *Hope of Heaven* (1938), it offers a
bonus. Here the regional perspective not only illumines but
helps to explain an otherwise inexplicable novel.

Following his first two praiseworthy novels—*Appointment
in Samarra* (1934) and *Butterfield 8* (1935)—*Hope of
Heaven*, O'Hara's only book-length treatment of Hollywood,
thoroughly dismayed the critics. Alfred Kazin called it "aimless," a book "smeared with glitter," and "woefully empty." [1]
Edmund Wilson, though crediting its "clean, quick and sure
style," found the novel disjointed, and one of its major characters, the young check-bouncer Don Miller, extraneous to
anything in the novel's apparent scheme.[2] In a more recent
study of O'Hara's fiction, Sheldon Grebstein dismisses *Hope
of Heaven* as supplying "no basis for prolonged consideration." [3] The book has been (to put it mildly) an unqualified
critical failure.

And failure it remains. No witnessing of the novel's affinity for the Southland, or for other Southland fictions, can
exculpate its singular deficiencies. But it can help to clarify
those deficiencies, and in doing so make clearer the novel's
intent. Once generally aware of the thematic and technical
inclinations encouraged by place, we can see in *Hope of
Heaven* many of the patterns and tendencies evident through-

out Southland fiction. Several of them are, apparently, the novel's most impelling motives.

More novella than novel, *Hope of Heaven*'s plot is fairly scant, and its characters, though emotionally more mobile than Cain's or McCoy's, are still less than fully credible people, even in the Hollywood milieu. Once again, however, we have in *Hope of Heaven* a Southland novel dominated not by character but theme: a novel whose central motif is that of dissolution, manifested particularly in breakdowns of identity, confusions of role, and sexual disorientation, and one whose primary significance, in spite of its realistic patina, is symbolic. Without specific reference to O'Hara, Frederick Bracher identifies the latter as a tendency of California writers toward "naïve symbolism," an inclination to impose allegoric meaning on characters "instead of finding significance in particular characters and events." [4] It is the tendency we have already seen at work personifying the collision of two sets of American values in a California hash house and metaphorizing American society's plight as a *danse macabre* on a rickety pier at Pacific's edge. One might reasonably speculate that the region's immense topography, diminishing man's sense of his own significance; its more than occasional unreality; and the human transience which so many observers have noted, together foster this tendency in the region's fiction toward symbolic narrative. It is at the symbolic level alone that *Hope of Heaven*'s characters and conflicts most nearly succeed as fiction. They work well enough at least to give the novel some basis for detailed, if not prolonged, consideration—as an allegory of dissolution.

Clearly, O'Hara intends his primary antagonists, Don Miller and the prodigal father Phil Henderson, to be read as symbolic doubles. His effort to establish a pattern of similarities between them would otherwise be inordinate. O'Hara's narrator, Jim Malloy (aged a bit since *Butterfield 8*, and now divorced) tells us that in "some respects, Philip Henderson was an older Don Miller." A generation between them, both are handsome, youthful-looking ne'er-do-wells. Both are drifters. Both men are college dropouts who had long before soured on middle-class aspirations. Both in the past had deserted their steady woman—women who both were kept by other men (Miller's girl by old Mossbacker the shirtmaker, Henderson's wife by her wealthy Pasadena benefactor who had begun providing for her after Henderson went to war). Both Miller and Henderson had become con men. Both had flirted with the wrong side of the law in money matters. And both have drifted unexpectedly into Los Angeles, locked in their anonymous conflict, into the lives of people with whom they had had scant contact long before. After fatefully affecting those lives with their conflict, both of them drift away unheard from again.

Those lives so severely affected by the Miller-Henderson tandem are lives which, prior to the two men's appearance, had achieved accommodation with the often lethal Southland milieu. To be sure, that milieu had exacted its toll on such as Malloy, Peggy Henderson, her brother Keith, and her friends Herbert Stern and Karen Waner. They all move within a framework of weakened values, loosened morals, and lost ideals. Nevertheless, new and at least nominally satisfying values have developed in their place, and with these diminished values each had come to terms with life and achieved personal equilibrium. There is even tenuous happiness.

Ultimately, however, that accommodation proves incapable of surviving the Southland's attraction for the Miller-Hendersons of America. From across the continent they both appear, first Miller, then Henderson, the one in flight, the other searching. In conflict over some stolen travelers' checks (things which themselves symbolize transience), the two men impose themselves upon the others, and in so doing shatter that accommodation. Their imposition begins innocuously when Miller introduces himself to Malloy and Peggy in the restaurant ("I do not like strangers who introduce themselves when I am having dinner with a girl," says Malloy). It ends profoundly with Henderson killing Keith. With the death of Keith, Malloy's and Peggy's world of accommodation comes apart.

At its most cogent level, the novel—like *Postman* and *They Shoot Horses*—is another fictional enactment, played upon the Southland stage, of the dissolution of the Great American Dream. Here it is a double dissolution. It is first a story of the Southland's corruption of that dream. One does not, as Henderson learned early, come to California to "grow up with the country." One comes to experience something else, something Herbert calls "the crystallization of the ordinary, cheap ordinary American." And it is a deterministic drama in which Malloy and Peggy and Keith, themselves a part of that crystallization, have their own new-found, Hollywood-reduced dream—shorn as it is of most traditional American values—destroyed by the chance intrusion of an anonymous conflict between two wandering con men, drifters with neither the time nor the inclination to adapt to the Southland ethos. The story parallels that of Cora Papadakis. Corrupted by Hollywood, then further corrupted by Frank, Cora still manages to build a new and less ambitious dream upon the ashes of the old. But that dream too, in an arbitrary act of fate, is snatched from her, and she is destroyed.

Stripped of its detail, O'Hara's little Hollywood allegory stands out rather clearly. But it is allegory wrought by an essentially unallegorical sensibility, by a writer with other talents and impulses demanding exercise in his work. O'Hara's eye for behavioral nuance, his ear for repartee, his impulse to play with the language and his love of effect, his concern over social matters, and his urge for psychological diagnosis all intrude into the novel and disorganize its form. These inclinations run roughshod over the novel's one reasonably unified dimension, its allegory of dissolution. They dominate it, obscure it, and in the end defeat it.

One human anomaly in particular engrosses O'Hara. It is a manifestation of breakdown reflected in virtually all Southland fiction (and soon after to be central to Nathanael West's *Day of the Locust*)—the corruption of love and normal sexuality. What Edmund Wilson sees as "a discernible but unfathomable Freudian behavior-pattern" in the novel is, in fact, the portrayal of an emancipated young woman newly stricken by emotional and sexual disorientation. It is established early that Peggy is a paragon of emotional stability. She is self-reliant, flagrantly independent, immovable in her convictions, and in full control of her emotional life. "I haven't got a good thinking brain," she tells Malloy, "but I have sound emotions." Then, her wayward father turns up, and her foundations are rocked. Only barely sublimated is the sexual attraction she feels for him. "What if I were on a train," she tells Malloy, calling it an idea for a shocking short story, "and . . . I let him pick me up and—so on. And he *is* at*tract*ive." [5]

Lest we miss the incestuous implication, O'Hara makes Peggy's comments quite clearly suggestive: "Then came the problem of where my father was going to sleep," she tells Malloy. "I'm glad he didn't stay the first night" (the one night Keith was unexpectedly absent). Her words echo with *double-entendre* ("What's he been doing all this time?" Malloy asks her. "I'll come to that," she replies). Complicating the problem is Keith's reaction to their father, and his own ambiguous relationship to Peggy. A loving younger brother, Keith is referred to by Peggy in terms more befitting a husband ("he didn't call up . . . and say he wasn't coming to dinner. As a rule he's very considerate about those things")—and a very jealous husband at that ("Change things! [He] certainly will change things, . . ." Keith says angrily to Peggy. "You and I have a nice home of our own, and . . . if he's planning to make our home his home, then I'm getting out"). As a result, Peggy, who had earlier refused to marry Malloy for sex or money, now, in order to placate a husbandlike brother and protect against her own attraction to a loverlike father, proposes to Malloy: "If he doesn't go away soon and if your offer is still good, I'll marry you," she tells him. "Or I'll live with you without getting married. I've just got to get away."

Some time later, lying in bed after lovemaking, Malloy and Peggy discuss her father. "He sometimes gives me the impression," she says, "that he thinks this is his home. Our house. And he's the father, and we're the children." Her remarks ring queerly, for Peggy and Malloy are bedded down in Malloy's house, not hers; she is talking to her lover, not her brother. Adding to Peggy's sexual-emotional disorientation is Malloy's admitted resemblance to her father, and the fact that he is "nearer her father's age and his kind of life than anyone Peggy knew. . . ." Henderson himself furthers the confusion later on by, in Malloy's words, "acting the stern parent" and reprimanding him for keeping Peggy out all night. This unexpected *stern*ness links Peggy's lover-father to the novel's other Stern, her slightly tubercular boyfriend Herbert, who is neither lover nor father-figure to Peggy. Karen Waner enters into the role confusion as little else than sexual alter-ego for Peggy. Karen has been Peggy's closest friend since school days; they were sexual initiates together. More overtly sensual than Peggy, Karen has nonetheless been emotionally wracked by her sexual experiences as Peggy (until now) has not. Karen, Peggy feels, would gladly give herself to Malloy if Peggy asked her to. It is over his father's sexual grab for Karen, this substitute Peggy, that Keith finally quarrels with and is accidentally killed by Henderson. "I guess he liked her," Henderson tells Malloy before leaving, "more than he ever let on."

Predictably then (when one understands what Peggy's attraction to Malloy had become), Peggy breaks their engagement after Keith's death and Henderson's departure. She no longer needs Malloy, or anyone in particular, as a substitute outlet for inexpressible incestuous impulses. In her last letter to Malloy, Peggy articulates as clearly as she can the cause of her distress (and there is no mistaking the suggestive import of her use of the word *intimately*):

> The trouble has been that you reminded me too much of my father, and at the same time you reminded me of Keith. I could not live with that combination. . . . When one of the three men I have known intimately in the past six months, kills the man I loved best in the world, the third man is unfortunately identified with the other two.

So ends O'Hara's tale of role-confusion and sexual breakdown. Possessed of the novel's only unambiguous set of affections, and deprived of their primary object, Malloy presumably takes up with a willing substitute, Karen Waner, as the story ends.

Not only in its allegorical and psychological frames, but in much of its detail, *Hope of Heaven* reflects the dissolution dominant in Southland fiction. Even the relatively stable Malloy provides an appropriately skewed point of reference. His divorce, like Henderson's, is a conventional correlative for the failure of love; and his relationship with Peggy, her own motives notwithstanding, is marked by a certain reversal of masculine and feminine: as Carolyn See has put it, "she leaves for work each morning to put in eight hours [while] he, a kind of hairy-chested harem queen, is left figuratively on a sofa with a box of bonbons; he has nothing to do but shop, and while away whole mornings picking out expensive neckties." [6] Sexual breakdown, one of the novel's dominant motifs, is also implied in the minor character who holds the keys to "home" in rootless Hollywood: Noel Sherman, the fairy desk clerk at Don Miller's hotel.

Tied as it is to implicit role-confusion, the novel abounds in explicit questions of identity. Its two antagonists, Miller and Henderson, each puzzle over the other's identity. "Don Miller? What Don Miller?" asks Henderson. "Who was the guy? . . . Who was he? . . . Who was this guy?" asks Miller when Malloy informs him of Henderson's interest in his name. Don Miller, it turns out, isn't really Miller's name— his real name is Schumacher. And he is "trying to get in the movies under the name of Don Mills." Schumacher finally admits that he remembers Malloy not as the older brother of a friend but as a local sportswriter back in Pennsylvania who had once *misspelled his name*. Malloy has trouble with Herbert's name too; he can never remember it. He addresses the waitress by a variety of names ("And the check, honey. Bobbie. Naomi. Betty. Ella. Check, please?"). Foreshadowing the breakdown of Peggy's emotional self-control, Malloy for the first time, once her father is in town, cannot recognize her voice over the phone. After she tells him of Henderson's arrival, Malloy asks her "What do you call him when you're with him?"

Malloy's Hollywood is a place where cops, rude and insensitive to things like grief, defer whenever someone flashes an "honorary detective's badge." It is a place where the rigor of the D.A.'s prosecutions depends not upon the criminal or the crime, or any notion of justice, but on proximity to election day. It is a town, as we see in Malloy's chat with the Broadway gambler, Red Luck, where it helps one's vital perceptions to have served time in prison, a place which attracts diminished moralities like that of Don Miller who can plead sincerely, "When I used to make a living playing pool I was always honest. Oh, I used to lose a couple games on purpose and then make the bets bigger, but that's business."

In adapting to this ethos, Malloy has shed the traditional values of his small-town past. When told by Peggy early in the story that she doesn't love him, doesn't even like him, he can ask "Well, why don't you marry me?" For Peggy, the traditional double standard is passé; she, not Malloy, calls the sexual shots. Courage, a most conventional virtue, is transformed in Hollywood into the kind of quality that makes charlatans like Don Miller "become Don Miller and stick to it." Even the subtropical Southland climate corrupts old values. "Christmas stank," Malloy tells us. "It doesn't have to be white for me to like it, but it ought to be reasonably cold, and there never ought to be palm trees." Peggy's radicalism serves the novel only to suggest a coping with society's broken values; no one else even takes it seriously.

Still other motifs of dissolution link *Hope of Heaven* to *Postman* and *They Shoot Horses*. A loss of reciprocal concern amongst people is suggested by Malloy's repeated references to "this Herbert" or "this Charlotte"; by his several anti-Semitic aspersions; and in his patronizing attitude toward Millie, the Henderson's Negro maid. The story also reflects the overriding importance of dollar value in Hollywood, the monetary motive that largely explains the accommodation of Malloy's ostensible writing talent to Hollywood demands. At the start we see him, feet on desk, "admiring my new $35 shoes, and my $7.50 socks, and thinking how nice it would be to go out and get in my $2200 car and go for a ride." The Christmas presents he buys are all itemized by cost. Even Herbert, the novel's young "intellectual"—for whom the effect of good piano is "too ephemeral" to be gratifying—wants the book he is writing to be "not a success d'estime, but a financial success." Even more clearly than in Cain or McCoy do we see language breaking down. Characters speak (and think) in cliché. Peggy spouts Marxist platitudes; Red Luck, Broadway jargon. Don Miller's talk is either frightened or banal, and riddled with solecism. Herbert's intellectualizing consists for the most part of painful commonplaces. Words lose their usual meanings. When Peggy tells Malloy "I'm not ready for another," he understands that she wants another drink. Through the din at the Beverly Brown Derby, we overhear a woman say ". . . I took opium," though we are sure she never did. The doctor at the hospital lies, telling Peggy that Keith has "about an even chance to live." Phil Henderson is compelled to euphemize his way around *speakeasy*, recalling his work with *restaurants*. In Red Luck's upside-down value system, "a larceny guy like me" is euphemism for *chiseller*. The salutation on Henderson's letters to Peggy and Keith, "Dear Kids, . . ." is a mockery of language, as, in another way, is Red Luck's double-talk routine in the restaurant.

Though less pervasively violent than either *Postman* or *They Shoot Horses, Hope of Heaven* does turn upon the accidental and deadly violence that Henderson wrecks on Keith. Two-dimensionality afflicts the most useful value standard in Malloy's Hollywood, as in Gloria Beatty's—not Gloria's ruthless distinction between success or failure, but the equally polarized distinction between *insider* and *outsider*. The novel's most destructive clashes are those between outsider and insider. The insiders (Malloy, Keith, and Peggy) want as little to do with the outsiders (Henderson and Miller) as possible. In minor incidents, we see the weight insiders carry in the Southland: Henderson foots the bill for their night out on the town, but it is Malloy who gets them into the Trocadero ("The head waiter's a friend of mine"). Red Luck is called upon for his insider's knowledge of the underworld fringes; but in Hollywood it is Malloy, there the insider, who can introduce Red to Loretta

Young, and by her nickname. The sense of constant motion and wasted energy so evident in *They Shoot Horses* is evident here too as Malloy, at the very beginning, tries unsuccessfully to get his "mind off the sound of the dynamo or the generator or whatever it was that made that sound. That sound never let up. . . . That sound is in every studio. . . . Some say it's a dynamo; some say it's the ventilator system; others say it's just water in the pipe-lines. Whatever it is, it's always near the writers' offices."

Among the novel's secondary motifs, those of illusion, façade, role-playing, and incongruity dominate its symbolic structure. The Henderson-Miller conflict is a series of identity confusions. Both men adopt deceptive guises. Miller boasts of how good an "appearance" he made back home in Swedish Haven, and he flaunts his facility at role-playing ("I can fool people into thinking I'm rich, and all I need is a few bucks and clothes. I just sit around and look wise"). As Malloy reconstructs Henderson's past, we learn how effective Henderson has been as a wheeling-dealing public relations man—as a maker of promotional images. Images of publicity and sales puffery dot the novel. Malloy's mail is loaded with promotional throwaways which he describes for us in detail. He envisions the cheap publicity he'll get when he and Peggy adopt some children. Peggy also plays roles: "All right," she tells Malloy. "But I'm a woman. Remember that. And I like to receive flowers. I may not *like* flowers, but—" At times, Malloy's perceptions, like Robert Syverten's, slip from reality into illusion. As Miller leaves him for the last time, Malloy recalls his "sitting in my room . . . like a frightened kid. . . . But the moment he left . . . he began to be different. Already I was *remembering* him. . . ." Before Miller leaves, Malloy cannot tell if his fright is routine or profound: "He put his face in his fingers and sat like a kibitzer or a condemned man." Façades assume disproportionate importance. O'Hara's descriptions of people are heavily sartorial. Malloy supposes that Peggy's antifascist meetings "don't do any harm" because "at least it shows the Fascists that we know they're having *their* meetings." Incongruity and confusion abound: the incongruity of

Christmas amid palm trees in hot weather; the confusion of finding one's way to the Hendersons' which took "at least half a dozen visits before you knew the way . . . [and] took a lot out of you to get there . . . you have to whirl your wheel continually all the way up. . . ." Peggy's proclivity for *non sequitur* only furthers this sense of confusion.

Like most Southland fictions, *Hope of Heaven* is rooted in a fatally deterministic world, a world whose unassuageable twists are consistent only in their irony. The novel's central irony is that Henderson and Miller, so remarkably alike, are pitted against one another in the narrative's most overt conflict. Ironic, too, is a crisis, which under normal conditions would likely bring two lovers closer together, driving a wedge of finality between them. On his deathbed, Keith adds to the novel's ironies, calling the shooting his fault. After his death, Peggy ironically prepares to prove her father's innocence.

More than Cain and less subtly than McCoy, O'Hara draws upon regional items and idiosyncrasies, such as the climatic incongruity of Christmas in Hollywood, for suggestive effect. The comparative remoteness of the hills north of Hollywood provides a contemplative escape ground for Peggy after Keith's death, a place outward and upward where her grief can be at least partly relieved, where she can take a more distant, "practical" view of her tragedy, and share with Malloy his Catholic's hope of heaven (another hope long before destroyed). In the hills, they climb beyond "the broken Hollywood land-sign"—a sign which still stands half-way up Mount Lee looking out over the basin—so clearly suggesting dissolution. O'Hara also parodies the scant and insular contents of the Los Angeles press to help characterize not only the city but, by his reactions to it, his narrator Malloy. "What's in the paper, Dad?" goes a local joke recalled by Malloy; "L.A. dog chases L.A. cat over L.A. fence." A culinary idiosyncrasy of region is used to suggest both Hollywood's provinciality and the speaker's banality: Isn't it "funny [Don Miller says] how in California the highest praise you can bestow upon a steak [is] to say that it [is] 'New York Cut.'" Malloy helps to characterize himself and his values by establishing his preferences among the images of various Hollywood personalities.

> To make up your mind to be something you're not, and to be it, and to be successful at being it—well, maybe Joan Crawford did want to hire a bross bond, but she made it. I'll take Mike Romanoff, and you can have Brian Ahearn. (But the trouble with all this is that you can also take the Lunts, and I'll take George Burns and Gracie Allen.)

And as he draws upon Hollywood, O'Hara also comments upon it; his Hollywood is subject as well as substance. Both directly and obliquely, the narrative passes judgment on the "fantastic, cheap, ordinary quality of Hollywood," its attractiveness to wandering thieves and con men, and its generally deleterious effect on the human spirit. The provinciality of Hollywood occupies much of the novel's commentary. Among the ironies in this irony-laden novel is the coexistence of this small-townishness with such rootlessness. The novel also provides brief sermons on "extramarital dabbling" in Hollywood, and on the almost parasitical existence of the Hollywood writer (a concern which later becomes central to the Hollywood fictions of Budd Schulberg and Scott Fitzgerald).

In all, then, there is evidence of some rather complex and subtle intention on O'Hara's part in *Hope of Heaven*—evidence that we see most clearly, I think, from a regional perspective. More than merely lacking a unified conception, as Edmund Wilson implies, the novel suffers from a pastiche of aesthetic objectives. It fails not because it is frivolous or insignificant, but because O'Hara's ambitions for it exceeded his ability to carry them off. Its deterministic allegory, the novel's solidest dimension, is overwhelmed by the failure of its pseudopsychology and by the very "clean, quick" style that Wilson praised. Peggy's carefully plotted Electral dilemma is less the subject of serious scrutiny than a kind of Chinese-ring puzzle whose interlocking parts fascinate and amuse us, but cause us to wonder no more than at the cleverness of the ring man. Her plight is less a case study for O'Hara than a word game, and a contrivance. Her problem is identified for us at Henderson's arrival, alluded to as deepening at a number of points in the narrative, then culminated in the throes of her personal crisis at the end— but never really shown us. The apparent complexity of Don Miller at the beginning also promises a serious study the novel never delivers. On the surface, *Hope of Heaven* is —as always with O'Hara—smoothly executed. Its style is built upon his eye for mannerism, his ear for repartee, and his concurrent experience as a movie scenarist. He plays for melodramatic effect in the dialogue of collusion between Malloy and Miller; for shock effect in Henderson's killing of Keith; and for laughs in the veritable stage routine, replete with double-talk, that Malloy and Red Luck conduct with the waitress, and in the numerous delightfully glib exchanges between Malloy and Peggy. But style clashes with substance. There is throughout a jarring incompatibility between the novel's narrative slickness, its allegorical dimension, and its fleeting gesture at serious psychology. Upon that clash, as much as anything else, *Hope of Heaven*—unlike McCoy's, or even Cain's, more elemental conceptions—comes hopelessly apart.

4

Shriek of the Locusts

Unquestionably, the most successful Hollywood novel of the 1930s — and since — is Nathanael West's *The Day of the Locust* (1939). With his earlier *Miss Lonelyhearts* (1933), it has been the subject of increasing and consistently favorable attention since West's rediscovery in the early fifties. The novel's success does, of course, concern us here. More specifically of interest, though, is the extent to which that success is effected by the influences (one is tempted, noting their recurrence, to call them imperatives) that seem wrought by the Southland region. Regional influence upon the novel's motifs, its tone, its narrative technique, upon its whole thematic conception, is indeed discernible. And its regional mosaic is more richly developed than we have seen it heretofore. It would be hard, in fact, to find a closer relationship between prose narrative and place than that between West's *Day* and Hollywood-Southland.

The novel's plot, an episodic sequence that opens one evening at the end of Tod Hackett's workday at National Films and ends months later in riotous chaos at a movie premiere, is, among other things, a drama of inexorable dissolution. In it, we witness an ongoing breakdown of human values, purpose, and dreams, with nothing but sordid emptiness left in their wake. And once again what is destroyed is expressly that collection of aspirations and impulses which constitute the Great American Dream. It is to "an American drummer" (the fundamental capitalist) that Faye Greener (West's heroine and the quintessence of Westian Holly-

wood) gives herself as a concubine in her first movie. Maybelle Loomis, single-mindedly ambitious for her little boy
Adore, is "eager and plump and very American." The pathetic Homer Simpson, trying to sing, knows only "The Star
Spangled Banner." That anthem's rockets may have cast an
inspiring red glare for Francis Scott Key at Fort McHenry,
but to Tod, running through a surrealist jumble of film sets
in pursuit of Faye, "the red glare in the sky" means something else: it "must be Waterloo" being filmed around the
bend. As West's personification of the Dream corrupted,
Faye Greener (her very name suggesting promise doomed)
is crass and vacuous, yet attractive like a flame to a swarm
of moths. In the painting Tod plans, "The Burning of Los
Angeles," it is Faye (and the Dream she represents) whose
nude form "throwing her knees high" like Saturday's ma-
jorette parading down Main Street is pursued by everyone
while the city burns. And it is she who survives. Tod Hackett, like Jim Malloy a man who can "hack it" and come to
terms with Hollywood, is only hurt in the chaos. The Homer
Simpsons are destroyed. West's Southland is not only the
Dream's most vivid dying ground; it is, as for McCoy, the
final one, the place where America physically ends, whence
there is no place left to run. It is the place, we are told repeatedly, where those from Des Moines and Sioux City come
to die, the same place where Gloria Beatty, after missing
her bus, walks with Robert "on down toward Western."

Much of the novel's intensity owes to West's repeated
compounding of this central theme. Not only is the Dream
itself corrupt, but its embodiment, Faye, is herself the victim
of frustrated dreams. She is an actress destined only for bit
parts, poorly played. (And Faye is not the novel's only emblem of hope destroyed: her father Harry, a former "Cam-
bridge Latin School pupil," is an ex-vaudevillean stumble-
bum headed for a pauper's grave until Faye's whoring buys
him a proper burial; Audrey Jenning, once a "fairly prom-
inent actress," now runs a whorehouse.) Even in her private
fantasies, where no one need fail, Faye is unable to choose
among the hackneyed plots she carries in her head. "While
she admitted . . . that it was better to slip into a dream

naturally, she said that any dream was better than no dream and beggars couldn't be choosers." [1] Compounding the frustration, the narrator tells us "she hadn't exactly said this," that Tod had to intuit it from what she did say. West also compounds our sense of the Great Dream's jadedness with successive reductions: we learn first how tough and calculating Faye is, then later that she is only seventeen; still later we see her with ribbons in her hair like a twelve-year-old; only to have the age of moral decay drop even further with the cruel-eyed, sexual gyrations of eight-year-old Adore Loomis—whose mother calls him "just a baby."

Among the breakdowns evident in the earlier novels, those that dominate West's are a corruption of traditional values, the death of love, and a perversion of normal sexuality. Values are such that Faye whores herself out—but not to Tod—precisely because "those men were complete strangers." After Tod adapts to Hollywood values, he finds Homer's qualities of resignation, kindliness, and humility annoying. Religion, that age-old repository of traditional values, becomes in the Southland a ridiculous collection of cults and sects, each with its "crazy jumble of dietary rules, economics, and Biblical threats." It is a young announcer at the premiere, with his "rapid, hysterical voice," who sounds "like a revivalist preacher whipping his congregation towards the ecstasy of fits." The traditional funeral ritual becomes instead a showcase for Mrs. Johnson's crass generalship: "You, Mrs. Gail," she bellows, "How about you? Don't you want a last look?" Even the climate (which ruined Malloy's Christmas) breeds irresponsibility; it encourages architectural chaos: "Steel, stone, and brick curb a builder's fancy a little, forcing him to distribute his stresses and weights and to keep his corners plumb, but plaster and paper know no law, not even that of gravity."

Love's death is clear throughout the novel, underscored by the statue of Eros on the back lot lying face downward "in a pile of old newspapers and bottles." Faye and Harry, Maybelle and Adore—the novel's only pairs of family members—disgrace any notion of familial love. The nearest thing to genuine affection in the novel is the dwarf Abe Kusich's trying tenderly to breathe life into the dying red cock, licking clear its eyes and desperately sucking blood back into its comb. Even here, of course, perversion is clearly suggested, the perversion which, of all the novel's breakdowns, predominates—that of normal sexuality.

Throughout the novel, sexuality is alternately confused, debased, and destroyed. The first time we see her, in a photo, Faye is dressed as a concubine and her legs are spread. But they are "swordlike legs." "Her invitation [isn't] to pleasure, but to struggle, hard and sharp, closer to murder than to love." Faye's gesture of running her tongue over her lips, which "seemed to promise all sorts of undefined intimacies," was really "as simple as the word thanks. She used it to reward anyone for anything, no matter how unimportant." Homer's hands, as Victor Comerchero has shown, repeatedly describe the motions of masturbation (the narrator frankly calls it "joint manipulation"); [2] and Homer is cloaked with the imagery of interrupted orgasm:

> He felt even more stupid and washed out than usual. It was always like that. His emotions surged up in an enormous wave, curving and rearing, higher and higher, until it seemed as though the wave must carry everything before it. But, the crash never came. Something always happened at the very top of the crest and the wave collapsed to run back like water down a drain, leaving, at the most, only the refuse of feeling.

Romola Martin, the object of Homer's earlier frustration, wears "a man's black silk dressing gown. . . . Her close cropped hair was the color and texture of straw and she looked like a little boy." Claude Estee's "drowned" rubber horse (a dead virility symbol) lies with its "hammerhead twisted to one side." Claude's party guests go to Mrs. Jenning's brothel not to have sex but to watch a film. In that film, *Le Predicamente de Marie*, the sumptuous young maid desires only the little girl. Piling frustration upon debasement, the film breaks down at the climactic moment. The brothel itself, where sex (however loveless) should flow gaily and freely, is instead a place where Mrs. Jenning "makes sex attractive by skillful packaging. Her dive's a triumph of industrial design." At the Cinderella Bar we not only see the flawless performance of a young female impersonator, but—in yet another of West's compoundings—we see him become, upon finishing his act, an "awkward and obscene" imitation of a man. During the brawl at Homer's, sex is symbolically (and wincingly) wrenched out of order as the dwarf rips at Earle Shoop's testicles. Significantly, in a novel so loaded with sexual implication, only a single affair is consummated—between Faye and Miguel—and even that is interrupted by Homer. West did indeed, as Comerchero says, seize upon sexual derangement as a crucial symptom of the failure of American society to provide emotional and spiritual gratification. But as we have seen, so too, in one way or another, did Cain, McCoy, and O'Hara. The region was rich with insistent examples.

And these dominant motifs of corruption in values, love and sexuality, are not the only ones shared by the novels. There are, for one, recurrent confusions of identity. The novel's one success symbol, Claude Estee, is a case in point. Living in "an exact reproduction of the old Dupuy mansion near Biloxi," he does impersonations that go with the architecture, and teeters "back and forth on his heels like a Civil War colonel, [making] believe he had a large belly [when, in fact, he] had no belly at all. . . ." Claude shouts to his butler, "Here, you black rascal! A mint julep," and a Chinese servant runs in with a scotch and soda. When Homer finally discovers Faye's true character in the bedroom with Miguel, she significantly pulls the sheets over her face. Like *Postman, Day of the Locust* also has its own anonymous Smith, the salesman to whom Faye, as a concubine, gives herself in her only movie.

Communication breaks down. Tod can exchange no more than a "Lo, thar" with Earle. Faye and Harry cannot even verbalize their quarrels—they must quarrel ritualistically, he laughing, she singing. Language itself falls apart. Traumatized by Faye's betrayal, it is Homer's language which most dramatically falters: he mumbles "gibberish. . . . The words went behind each other instead of after. . . . long strings were really one thick word and not a sentence." Throughout the novel, inarticulate characters take recourse in songs and in ritual dancing—a motif which Randall Reid has described in detail.[3] Another breakdown of language, as in the novels we have looked at earlier, is the frequent and in some cases total dependence of West's characters on cliché. Faye incessantly talks in platitudes ("Luck is just hard work, they say . . ."); she picks up her most "picturesque" language from the chatter column of a Hollywood trade paper; and fantasizes "original" movie plots out of towering clichés. Abe Kusich and Earle Shoop are both linguistically stunted, limited to the stereotyped argot of the racetrack tout and the rawboned cowpoke. For Harry Greener, life itself has been a round of five-a-day vaudeville routines describable only through a show-business code language: "a lightning series of 'nip-ups,' 'high-gruesomes,' 'flying-w's,' and 'hundred-and-eights' done to escape a barrage of 'exploding stoves.' "

Constituted authority fares no better with West than with Cain, McCoy, or O'Hara. It is either corrupt or impotent. Tod implies that the police took protection payoffs at his apartment on Ivar. During the riot, the police are barely tolerated by the mob, tolerated "as a bull elephant does when he allows a small boy to drive him with a light stick." In turn, the cops "good-naturedly" lead a man away "until they got him around the corner [and] whaled him with their clubs."

Art, too, has broken down in this place where architecture is designed not to please but to startle. Tod, the artist, loses pleasure in composition and color, and goes the way of his classmates "towards illustration or mere handsomeness." His painting, "The Burning of Los Angeles," never does get painted. In one of the novel's most jarring images, the boorish Mrs. Johnson raises her hand at Harry's funeral and silences Bach "in the middle of a phrase." Preempting art once again is the money motive. The *Waterloo* actors are overjoyed when their canvas hill collapses; they "were certain to receive several extra days' pay, and the man with the ught he might get as much as five hundred

ploys some of the same ethnic prejudices we

have seen earlier, using them to objectify a generalized demise of human relationships. At the Cinderella Bar, Tod comments that "only a Negro could have worn [Homer's outfit] without looking ridiculous." Among the minor characters are a family of grunting Eskimos. The novel's aboriginal American is the absurd Chief Kiss-My-Towkus who (in only one of the novel's numerous anti-Semitic gestures) flaunts a Yiddish accent. The men at Claude's party wonder how they can "get rid of the illiterate mockies that run the movie industry." The huge electric sign which looms ironically over the riot—MR. KAHN A PLEASURE DOME DECREED—besides echoing the "phantom-world" of Xanadu (and functioning sexually as we'll see in a moment), also parodies a Jewish idiom, and alludes to the grinning face of Ikey Cohn, symbol of New York's Rockaway Playland. At the cockfight, the cock named *Juju* slashes and stabs the slower *Hermano* (brotherhood) and finally gaffs it through the brain.

Human decay and dissolution are also evident in West's Hollywood. Claude Estee is a "dried up little man with . . . rubbed features and stooped shoulders." Joan Schwartzen, the champion tennis player (who was to have been a seven-foot lesbian in an earlier version of the novel), has an eighteen-year-old face sitting on a "thirty-five-year-old neck that was veined and sinewy." Homer's eyes finally become "empty of everything, even emotion."

Among the novel's motifs, one of the most striking is its characters' persistent willingness, even enthusiasm, for corruption and destruction. Though admitting Faye's artificiality, Tod is "anxious for it to succeed." Not only do hoards of outsiders come, lemminglike, to their deaths in California but the lethargic Homer (who is one of them), once fully afflicted by Hollywood's force (by Faye's deception and Adore's violent taunting), himself turns violent and, in so doing, is consumed by the mob. In a sense, the death wish that marked Gloria Beatty and Robert Syverten as Hollywood insiders, and the impulse that drove Keith Henderson to attack his obviously armed father, overtakes Homer as well. And his new-found abandon kills him in minutes.

The array of secondary motifs apparent in the earlier

novels—those patterns of imagery and symbol reinforcing
the dominant dissolution motif—is also evident in West's,
and much more richly than before. Violence is frighteningly
routine, dominating the novel from its intimations of im-
minent battle on the opening page to the garish mob bru-
tality of the closing chapter. And it is senseless violence
staged for an American readership West thought accustomed
to it: European writers, he said, have "to do a great deal of
careful psychology and sociology . . . to motivate one little
murder. But not so the American [whose] audience . . . is
neither surprised nor shocked if he omits artistic excuses for
familiar events." [4] Before the cockfight, Abe and Earle exchange taunts as meaningless as they are vicious. Claude
Estee buys one of the birds simply to see a cockfight. Earle
clubs Miguel for dancing with Faye, and later kicks Abe for
cutting in when Faye and Miguel are dancing. The epic
battle in *Waterloo* is utterly wasted as the scaffolding collapses (resulting nonetheless in widespread injury). West
underscores the routineness of violence with a masterfully
understated sentence at the encampment: "Earle caught the
birds one at a time and pulled their heads off before drop-
ping them into his sack." During the climactic riot, the
narrator explains that "nothing can ever be violent enough
to make taut [these people's] slack minds and bodies."

That riot also makes clear, were it not so already, that
violence in West's Hollywood—as in Cain's, McCoy's, and
O'Hara's—is largely sexual, a libidinal dam giving way under
the pressure of constrained and frustrated yearnings. The
final chapter's intensely symbolic narrative, in image after
phallic image, prepares for, builds toward, and finally erupts
into frenzied orgasm, discharging its violence in waves which
churn through the welling mob on Hollywood Boulevard.
The scene opens with "a dozen great violent shafts of light"
sweeping crazily across the evening sky over the "Pleasure
Dome" (one almost expects its roof to be haired). The crowd
in front of it, whose members individually lack "the physical
equipment for pleasure," *en masse* form an excited and volatile "thick line" impatiently waiting at its entrance. The
theater's "rose-colored domes and delicate minarets" are un-

mistakably those of a female body—but a body to be entered only by celebrities, not by the mob. As the thick line grows, the police enforce a separation between crowd and theater. Then Homer appears at the edge of the crowd, drifting catatonically with a piece of his nightgown hanging out his open fly like a flannel penis between the two suitcases he is carrying. Intercepting him, Tod leaves Homer on a bench momentarily, thinking it will still be awhile before the crowd "overran" it. From behind the trunk of a tall tree, however, little Adore Loomis tempts Homer with a purse on a string—a ragged and fly-infested purse, a befouled female receptacle. When Adore's tempting turns to taunts, then violent assault (hurling his rock in Homer's face), Homer rises up, incensed, "like a stone column," and overwhelms him. The anxious crowd, constrained from entering the theater, suddenly turns its impatient frenzy away from the Pleasure Dome entrance and rushes Homer. Overrun by the mob, Homer, the stone column with a silent, "open mouth," rises above the mass for a moment, then is pulled down. Attempting to aid him, Tod is caught up in this ejaculatory metaphor. In the "dizzy rush," he "closed his eyes and fought to keep upright." During "wild surge" after surge— each ending "in a dead spot where the pressure was less"— Tod witnesses the orgasmic reactions of people in the mob: sobbing young girls, squealing women, a neck-biting old man. Hurt but alive, Tod sees the details of his painting rush through his mind. The canvas is framed with the flames of his prophesied Los Angeles conflagration—flames which "lick . . . avidly at [the] corinthian column . . . of a nutburger stand."

The riot's climactic juxtaposition of sex and violence has, of course, been prepared for all along. Little Adore's song and dance carry a "top-heavy load of sexual pain." To get Claude's bird to fight more effectively, Abe scratches its testicles. Faye's open legs are swordlike. The ecstatic moans Homer hears from Faye's bedroom he takes to be those of pain. Earle Shoop, the vacuous stud, stands habitually in front of a saddlery window that displays "a large collection of torture instruments." The hen that Miguel keeps for the pleasure of his cocks has its feathers torn from its neck, its comb is bloody, and its feet are full of scabs—and Faye tells Homer "it's only natural." Even Tod, West's normal young protagonist, converts his yearning for Faye into impulses to throw her into the mud and (like Frank Chambers) taste the blood in her lips, to break her smooth self-sufficiency with a blow, and later, simply to club her with a bottle and rape her. The link between sex and cruelty does indeed color virtually every episode in the novel.

The "two-dimentional" motif also assumes a major role in *Day of the Locust*. Its characters are, for the most part, two-dimensional caricatures, pathetic or sordid puppets set into motion by West to enact the Great Dream's breakdown. Even Tod, ironically described by West as "a very compli-cated young man," never really demonstrates any breadth of character. Like McCoy, West not only deals in the two-dimensional; he cultivates it. Adore bows, clicks his heels, and turns like a soldier at the command of his drill-sergeant mother. Abe Kusich, when he laughs, uses "only two notes, ha-ha and ha-ha, over and over again." Harry Greener's face has lost its capacity for subtle expression: "like a mask," it is a face that "wouldn't permit degrees of feeling, only the farthest degree." Earle Shoop has "a two-dimensional face that a talented child might have drawn with a ruler and a compass," and his behavior is the kind that goes "from ap-athy to action without the usual transition." West's charac-ters also reflect the same polarity of naïf and initiate we have seen before; his focal character, Tod, moves from one pole to the other during the novel. And characteristically, West's characters polarize compoundedly: they are also, on one hand, the "masqueraders" constantly in motion on Vine Street and, on the other, somber and disheveled loiterers, starers and haters, who have come to California to die. Tod makes it clear that survival depends upon one's adapting to the two-dimensional: overhearing the dwarf's laugh, Tod advises Homer, "You could learn from him." The two-dimensional motif extends beyond the novel's characters. Tod's search for Faye through stage sets from ancient Troy to the 14th Street "El" is a sustained encounter with two-

dimensional reality. Passing through the s
the Last Chance Saloon, Tod finds himsel
at the end of which stands a Romanesque
lawn of fiber, a group of men and wo
cardboard food in front of a cellophane

Façade, deception, and the playing of
motifs. The homes of Hollywood, from the rows of smaller
houses "all of plaster, lath, and paper," to Claude Estee's
mock plantation, are all essentially façades. Vice at Mrs.
Jenning's is made attractive "by skillful packaging." Funeral
chapel decor consists of "imitation stained-glass windows
which hung on . . . fake oak-panelled walls." Faye's beauty,
such as it is, is wholly external, "structural like a tree's."
Actors, in general, are mostly personified façades: "Harry,
like many actors, had very little back or top to his head. It
was almost all face" Mrs. Johnson's interest in funerals is
strictly "the arrangement of the flowers, the order of the
procession, the clothing and deportment of the mourners."
The men at Claude's party want an industry foundation, like
the Rockefeller, to improve the image of the image-making
industry: "You know, give the racket a front."

And deception is rife. Harry Greener takes a reviewer's
pan, and twists it into a blurb for himself in *Variety*. The
real estate agent promises Homer he will "see doves and
plumed quail" in Pinyon Canyon; "all the time he lived
there, he saw only a few large, black velvet spiders and a
lizard." Disingenuousness abounds. For all her apparent
squeamishness over the quail traps, Faye eats as heartily as
the men. In swallowing his drink, Harry makes all the faces
that go with medicine, then quickly pours himself another.
Joan Schwartzen derides the game of tennis; then we learn
she is a tennis champion. Even the crowd plays roles: when
the radio announcer hollers "here, listen to them roar," those
near the microphone "obligingly roared for him."

The role-playing motif recurrent in Southland fiction becomes central to West's Hollywood vision. In West's hands
the motif is epitomized, pushed as far as it will go in repeated
defiance of our disbelief. Harry Greener's every moment is an
ongoing role, and very badly played. Claude Estee, to make

tations *less* ridiculous, adds a mock flourish when he
s to Faye. Under Faye's influence, even Homer plays the
ole of gracious host, making "a little set speech about
everybody coming in for a drink" after the cockfight which
sickens him. He also pretends to enjoy the brandy force-fed
him by Faye at the Cinderella Club. Playing roles is, of
course, a means of survival in West's Hollywood; and
Comerchero is correct in claiming that Homer cannot really
play a role.[5] Ultimately, Homer cannot sustain the roles he
is fleetingly forced to play, and as a result is destroyed.

Inseparable from motifs of façade, pretense, and the
playing of roles, here as elsewhere, is the novel's frequent
juxtaposition of reality and illusion. People on Vine Street
"wore sports clothes which were not really sports clothes."
Homer's house is gumwood painted to look like fumed oak,
its "hand-forged" hinges are carefully stamped by machine,
its thatched roof is "not really straw but heavy fireproof
paper colored and ribbed to look like straw." Some of
Homer's cacti are rubber and cork, others are real. Faye's
mourning garment is a tattered black negligee, and in it she
gives off a warm, sweet odor. Her conversational gestures do
not illustrate what she is saying. At one point during his
seizure, Harry doesn't know himself whether he is sick or
acting. The young male transvestite turns out to be more
woman than man. The novel's most garish juxtaposition of
reality and illusion is the ludicrous rubber horse in Claude
Estee's pool. With it, though, West means to show us
something more of illusions—the extent to which people
desire and cling to them. Joan Schwartzen thinks Tod a
"meanie" for recognizing the hoax: "You just won't let me
cherish my illusion," she says reproachfully. Her cherished
illusions are, of course, little different from those of "the
barber in Purdue," who, as Claude says, "doesn't want [in a
movie] to see some dope carrying a valise or fooling around
with a nickel machine. What the barber wants is amour
and glamour."

Tied again to this reality-illusion motif are numerous
flashes of incongruity, from the little man with the mega-
phone chasing an army across a sound stage, to the bizarre

sexual assaults during the riot. We see the Indian chief with a Yiddish accent; the world-weary Faye with a little-girl bow in her hair; a neighborhood where Samoan hut, Mediterranean villa, Japanese temple, and Swiss chalet are scattered randomly over the hills; the testimonials on Abe's business cards ("the Lloyd's of Hollywood. . . ." "Abe's word is better than Morgan's bonds . . ."); Abe's helping to get the slut's fiddle out of hock; and a score of other incongruities no less jarring.

Apparent too is the kinetic speed-up evident in the earlier novels. Harry's frenetic "routine" in Homer's living room, as Jay Martin puts it, is like "a film run too rapidly," altering human rhythms into mechanical ones.[6] West's Angelenos are not only self-destructive but a suicidal avant-garde: they "would be first [to die] . . . their comrades all over the country would follow."

And those crowds of Angelenos, like the crowds at McCoy's marathon, are contemptible and brutish. They are an organic "dense mass," a vicious phallic collective "surg-[ing] forward wherever the police line was weakest. As soon as [one] part was rammed back, the bulge would pop out somewhere else." West's crowds are pariahs, watching planes at the airport and waiting for a crash, following funerals and "hoping for a dramatic incident of some sort, hoping at least for one of the mourners to be led weeping hysterically from the chapel." And they are corrupters, these "lower middle classes," who cheapen art in a way which both accommodates and cheats the corrupters. West typifies his crowd-man as a "worshipper" at the Tabernacle of the Third Coming, a hick from Sioux City who

> had the same countersunk eyes, like the heads of burnished spikes, that a monk by Magnasco might have. He was probably just in from one of the colonies in the desert . . . conning over his soul on a diet of raw fruits and nuts. He was very angry. The message he had brought to the city was one that an illiterate anchorite might have given decadent Rome. It was a crazy jumble of dietary rules, economics, and Biblical threats. He claimed to have

seen the Tiger of Wrath stalking the walls of the citadel and the jackal of Lust skulking in the shrubbery, and he connected these omens with "thirty dollars every Thursday" and meat eating.

West had a theory, a friend recalls, that the people who lined up at Grauman's early in the morning to worship the stars as they arrived, really hated them and longed to tear them to pieces, to shred their flesh as much as their clothes.[7] West's crowds are his titular locusts descending *en masse* upon the Southland—as Don Miller and Phil Henderson do *en deux*—and by their very presence, destroying.

Comerchero's contention that the novel is almost devoid of irony seems unjustifiable.[8] Like the Southland corpus in general, it is heavily ironic, its irony an intriguing mixture of the subtle and the heavy-handed. West's treatment of Tod, his central character, is ironic from beginning to end. "Despite his appearance," he says of Tod, "he was really a very complicated young man with a whole set of personalities, one inside the other like a nest of Chinese boxes"—boxes which, West need not have added, must all be empty to fit. In the very next sentence, Tod's yet-to-be-painted picture somehow "prove[s] he had talent." All that Tod ever does complete of his prophetic painting is a series of preliminary "cartoons" and some "rough charcoal strokes." During the riotous climax, we see in that still unpainted picture that Tod, who had begun as a disinterested observer-critic of Los Angeles, has ironically become one of the rock throwers.

The novel is replete with ironic tableaux: the congregation of raging cultists singing Christian hymns, Faye's daintily curled finger at the end of her voraciously devoured meal, her preoccupation with a pimple while Harry lay dead on the couch behind her (recalling Frank and Cora's preoccupying carnality alongside Nick's dead body). Aspirations in the novel are ironic, like Claude Estee's aspiration to be a plantation master, a thoroughly decadent life-style. And history speaks out ironically in the person of the Indian, most cheated of all by the American Dream, now become a phony commercial instrument hawking his own tradition. West's irony, as Randall Reid has noted, enters even into the novel's structure in the mock-Euripidean movement of the novel's climax, with the disproportionate fury of its bacchantes and their torches about to fire the palace. The irony here, notes Reid, is not in the contrast between an exalted classic tradition and West's trivial characters, but between the triviality of those characters and the demonic forces within them.[9] *Day of the Locust* unquestionably speaks the ironic voice of Southland fiction.

It also reflects the unabashed moralism of Southland writers, and their consistently deterministic point of view—with West's perhaps the bleakest determinism of them all. (Fitzgerald felt that the novel put Gorky's *Lower Depths* "in [a] class with *The Tale of Benjamin Bunny*.") [10] West the moralist was a man who scorned the Catholic Church for its hypocrisies and its economics, a man who "had so much heart," his secretary recalls, "that he was a sucker for any cause." He strongly disapproved of Hollywood's sexual mores, and was indignant over John O'Hara's use of a young woman they both knew as his model for Peggy Henderson. This moralistic impulse is incorporated into his self-derisive alter ego, Tod Hackett. Tod, like West an artist *cum* Hollywood social critic, turns away from decorative artists like Winslow Homer and Ryder to embrace bitter social critics like Goya and Daumier. He lusts after Faye, but refuses to pay for her at Mrs. Jenning's. He is, as Reid calls him, an insistent moralist, a man "afflicted with a moral impulse whose traditional forms have collapsed"—impotent, but insistent.[11]

The hyperbole frequent in other Southland novelists becomes unrelieved in West. More deftly controlled than the hyperbole of *Postman* (and far more tolerable where no bid is made for our sympathies), the novel's audacious overstatement is among its great strengths. And West knew it. "If I put into *Day of the Locust*," he said, "any of the sincere, honest people who work here and are making such a great progressive fight, these chapters couldn't be written satirically and the whole fabric of the peculiar half-world which I attempted to create would be badly torn by them." [12] West's cackling whores, his suicidal fornications, his drooling worshippers and stick-sucking old men are all the hyperbolic stuff with which he builds his novel. Hyperbolic, too, is the kind of image magnification we saw in Robert Syverten's stethoscopic sensitivity to the ocean tide. Here it is Homer's hands, those frustrated, masturbatory, alien hands West returns to repeatedly as they reflect and intensify the heat, the cold, and the itch of Homer's subconscious. The whole enervating ethos of West's Southland demands exaggeration, like the foods in his market which demand colored spotlights to heighten their natural hues.

Beyond its themes, its motifs, and its tone, the novel's narrative technique ties it even closer to the regional corpus. Though not technically a first-person narrative (as each of our other novels is), its essential outlook is nonetheless that of its protagonist, Tod Hackett, the artist-critic of the Hollywood milieu. Significantly, West's original conception of the novel *was* that of a first-person narration by Claude Estee, whose role in the ultimate version becomes substantially reduced. By the final draft, West was resisting an actual first-person voice, not only to more expediently narrate the more private of the Homer Simpson chapters (chapters 8 through 12) but to give himself the fluidity of a Joycean third-person narrator, the narrative posture that Saul Bellow was to adopt so successfully, with its capacity to slide at will from an omniscient, nearly total identification with one's protagonist to a sudden and sometimes startling ironic distance. West's' narrative perspective in *Day of the Locust,* then, is a reflection of his maturing as a novelist, the rejection of a regionally encouraged first-person perspective in favor of the better, more flexible way of telling his ironic yet intensely experienced story.

It is also a highly visual novel, focusing with special intensity on colors and shapes. Abe's Tyrolean hat, more befitting a wicked gnome than a track tout, is "the proper magic green color and had a high, conical crown." At the foot of Pinyon Canyon, where reality and artifice so often clash, the "edges of the trees burned with a pale violet light and their centers gradually turned from deep purple to black." The same neonlike piping, like the violet light which bathes the unreal city of Eliot's *Waste Land*, outlines the tops of the "ugly humpbacked hills" that surround West's Hollywood. Colors are clashed to evoke the town's garishness: the façade of the San Bernardino Arms is "the color of diluted mustard and its windows [are] framed by pink Moorish columns." It is, after all, a visual conception which frames the entire novel —Tod's vision of "The Burning of Los Angeles."

Like other Southland fictions, the novel's structure is decidedly episodic, a structure which James Light, among others, feels is strongly suited to depictions of falseness and "surrealistic grotesqueness." Light attributes the novel's "swiftly changing settings" and its "roving, panoramic technique" to West's training as a screenwriter.[13] After fleeting glimpses of the back lot, of Sunset Boulevard, and the city's architectural hodgepodge at the book's beginning, we are whisked through a mock-scenario by Claude Estee, a showing of *Le Predicamente de Marie*, and a reviewer's brisk description of Harry's vaudeville routine. The sensation is that of a rapid-fire series of one-reelers. This scenariolike structure is, in fact, one of the few things that has troubled critics. George Milburn, from whom West expected an unqualified rave, said in the *Saturday Review*: "The worst part of the book is that it follows the choppy, episodical technique of a movie scenario. It has that peculiar disorganization that most movies have." [14] More recently, Comerchero has called the novel diffuse, lacking in compression.[15] Avoiding critical judgments, Jay Martin concludes—and quite correctly I think —that "photography and the film clip" are the basis of both style and structure in *Day of the Locust*.[16]

An intensely regional novel, *Day of the Locust* draws even more heavily than the earlier novels upon idiosyncrasies of place for aesthetic effect. The regional item most strikingly employed in the novel—and I suspect unsurpassably—is the Hollywood set. As literary device, its suggestive potential is endless. It can be made to represent any place, any time, anything, and—in its impermanence—any fate can befall it for the slightest or most whimsical of causes. Tod's search for Faye through the studio lot becomes an odyssey through an absurd, symbolic wonderland unbounded by time or space.

This journey, more than anything else in the novel, universalizes West's prophecy of doom for Western civilization. Once Tod passes through all the current sets, we are prepared for, even anticipating, the gigantic pile of discarded ones, the ever-growing mountain of flats and props which constitute West's "dream dump," his "Sargasso of the imagination."

The site of the dream dump, "a ten-acre field of cockleburrs spotted with clumps of sunflowers and wild gum," is only one of the novel's numerous uses of indigenous flora. The cockleburr (like the cockleburr that opens Steinbeck's "turtle" interchapter in *Grapes of Wrath*) suggests a passive but armed and hostile environment awaiting the naïve trespasser. The clumsy sunflower parodies the Southland's most heralded virtue, its omnipresent sun. (Later on we are told expressly "the sun is a joke.") The wild gum, like the gum-wood door of Homer's cottage, hints at the tenacious grip the Southland ethos has upon those attracted to it. Behind the lot, Tod sees live oak and cactus straight out of Salvatore Rosa, the former silently enacting a sexual agony: "great, tortured trees, whose exposed roots writhed dramatically in the arid ground." West repeatedly turns to cactus—with its "armories of spikes, hooks, and swords"—as a natural symbol for tenuous survival in this arid environment, and as a phallic reminder. He combines long shot with close-up of the California poppy to heighten our sense of the discrepancy between bright illusion and deathly reality: "Orange poppies bordered the path [along the canyon floor]. Their petals were wrinkled like crepe and their leaves were heavy with talcum-like dust." West's people are bored by the succulence of fresh oranges in this jaded region. Even avocado, mythical aphrodisiac, fails to arouse them. The bicolored eucalyptus leaf—leaf of the tree emblemizing a school of regional celebrants in painting—is used by West to suggest the monetary icon of Hollywood: "A light breeze stirred its . . . . leaves . . . . show[ing] first their green side, then their silver one." The unmistakable form of the towering date palm, for Robert Syverten like a grotesque sentry, is doubly suggestive in West's hands. Coming out of Homer's the night of the cockfight, Tod "had to sit down on the curb with his back against a date palm." When the image is repeated, ". . . Tod frowning, his back pressed hard against the palm tree," we realize that this peculiar Southland flora, its sweet promise far overhead and out of reach, has become a substitute spine, Tod's only support amidst the degeneracy which surrounds him.

Among regional fauna, West employs the lizard struggling for survival in Homer's cactus garden while Homer watches over it, an impotent God. And he uses the California thrush —"that bird that sings at night in California"—as an image of inverted reality, "bursting its heart" melodramatically "in runs and quavers" while Tod imagines himself raping Faye.

A canyon climb, through the Westian eye, becomes a journey into a sterile vagina no less treacherous than Faye's. Tod, Faye, and Earle make their Freudian climb

> until they reached another canyon. This one was sterile, but its bare ground and jagged rocks were even more brilliantly colored than the first. The path was silver, grained with streaks of rose-grey, and the walls of the canyon were turquoise, mauve, chocolate, and lavender. The air itself was vibrant pink.

Once in the canyon, they watch a hummingbird chase a blue jay in a mocking reenactment of fertilization, mocking because its results are so flamboyantly inconsequential:

> The jay flashed by squawking with its tiny enemy on its tail like a ruby bullet. The gaudy birds burst the colored air into a thousand glittering particles of metal confetti.

The coital motif continues as they exit the canyon:

> When they came out of this canyon, they saw below them a little green valley thick with trees, mostly eucalyptus [its characteristic smell that of tomcat spray], with here and there a poplar and one enormous black live-oak.

—at journey's end, a blackened phallus.

Among regional phenomena, West employs a nighttime sky crisscrossed by kleig lights, shafts of light used to herald the public opening of everything from motion pictures to gasoline stations. He draws upon the region's rampant cultism (West was at once fascinated and repelled by movements like the Townsendites and Aimee MacPherson's Angelus Temple which flourished during the late 1930s). He features an old silent-screen star who couldn't make it in talkies (Audrey Jenning recalling the actor Emil Jannings likewise victimized by his foreign accent). Mrs. Jenning's brothel is drawn after Lee Francis's, well known to Hollywood insiders at the time. The Cinderella Bar is also an actual and well-known night spot. The proximity of city streets to canyon wilds, so amazing to Southland newcomers, furthers the novel's reality-illusion motif. Even the assortment of dreams on file in Faye's mind takes its inspiration from the files of "original" story ideas kept on hand at every studio and consulted by scenarists whenever the well ran dry.

Scenes in the novel which seem to owe entirely to the lurid Westian imagination are all the more effective when one learns their debt to Hollywood reality. West's friend and fellow novelist, Allan Seager, recalls (with delightful *double-entendre*) that the "saddle shop with the hitching racks in front where [Earle Shoop] hung out was just across from the old KNX radio station on Sunset. No horse was ever hitched to the racks but I have seen the movie cowpunchers sitting on them by the hour." [17] Another friend recalls West's coming home one night and the door opposite his apartment bursting open. One of the prostitutes who lived there cursed and kicked something out of the door that looked like a bundle of dirty laundry—until the bundle got up and walked off. West used the incident to introduce Abe Kusich; and he modeled him on a well-known dwarf who peddled papers at Hollywood and Wilcox. [18]

West uses Hollywood profusely, and he indicts it brutally. His Hollywood is the corrupt residue of America's manifest destiny, a "pleasure dome decreed" which became instead the graveyard of the Great American Dream. It is a place whose walking embodiment, Faye Greener—like decadent medieval artists before her—feels that fantasy is made plausible by realistic and humdrum details. It is a place which, like another of its Westian personifications, Abe Kusich, is grotesque and depraved in its stuntedness, a place as tinny as Abe's high-pitched cackle, but a place which, like Abe, has "a powerful grip." West paints a place (and unlike Tod, completes his painting) which is magnet and receptacle for legions of drifters, kooks, and perverts—a judgment on region more or less implied in every Southland novel we have looked at so far. His Hollywood people—the affluent and the common—like the movie-watchers at Mrs. Jenning's, all thrive on the lusts and perversions of others and "riot" when the film breaks down. Success in West's Hollywood is an imitation house, with a swimming pool full of illusions. Failure is, at first, realization that the pleasure dome does not work, then boredom, apathy, rage, and finally death.

Though West's stature as a writer has, for the most part, been posthumously accorded, *Day of the Locust* did not lack for praise upon publication (nineteen months before West's death). Fitzgerald's praise was the most satisfying to West, but far from its only. Though critical of structure, George Milburn thought Tod's journey through the dream dump comparable only to Stephen Dedalus's vision of Hell.[19] Jack Conroy, in the radical *Progressive Weekly*, called West "one of America's most brilliant satirists." [20] In his *New Republic* review, Edmund Wilson called the novel a "remarkable book," praised it for catching "the emptiness of Hollywood," and for "mak[ing] this emptiness horrible." [21]

To be sure, the novel is not without flaw. West's ironic treatment of Tod (a self-derisive irony aimed at his own alter ego) lessens Tod's effectiveness as an observer of the ironies which surround him. The narrative suffers a bit from ironic overkill. Its characterizations, most notably Claude Estee, are at times inconsistent. Elsewhere, as in its introduction of Faye, we are forced to take West's word on characters before seeing them in action. Some of the novel's value judgments, however warranted their stridency, are too obvious and too early. Not three pages into the narrative are we told that "only dynamite would be of any use against" Hollywood architecture. And some of the novel's imagery— like the stick-sucking man, and Homer's infantile force-feeding by Faye at the Cinderella Bar—is a bit forced even in the novel's unsubtle context. But these are flaws of excess in a novel of excess, a novel intended to shock us with the audacity of its portraiture, a novel which does not measure good against bad, or bad against worse—but where all is nightmare. They are minor flaws in a major fictional achievement, an achievement which owes inestimably to region.

5

Grey Knight in the Great Wrong Place

Raymond Chandler's fiction has more than once provoked
the question of categories. Though a self-proclaimed writer
of murder and detection stories, Chandler was not, so Edmund Wilson argues, writing an "old-fashioned detective
novel," but rather a "novel of adventure," a novel conveying
not so much a puzzle as a malaise.[1] W. H. Auden goes
further, calling Chandler's efforts "not detective stories, but
serious studies of a criminal milieu, the Great Wrong Place,
which should be read and judged, not as escape literature,
but as works of art." [2] Except for *Little Sister* (1949), Chandler's novels are not often thought of as Hollywood fiction.
No writer of fiction, though, is felt more to convey the
essence of Los Angeles—a distinction which our hypothesis
seeks, if not to obliterate, at least to minimize. Chandler
does indeed draw upon much of the same Southland region
of the 1930s (and after) that West, O'Hara, Cain, and
McCoy do; and out of it he shapes that ethos Auden calls
the Great Wrong Place. Chandler uses the Southland region
as a living, heterogeneous entity in his fiction, and that
complex organism correspondingly helps to shape the Chandler aesthetic. Whatever claim other categories may lay,
Chandler's fiction does exhibit those characteristics of theme
and motif, of attitude and style (modified of course to the
Chandlerian vision) that have earlier been identified as the
aesthetic dimensions of Hollywood-Southland fiction.

Though any of Chandler's better novels would serve, his
second, *Farewell, My Lovely* (1940), the novel most often

judged his finest, is as good a work as any in which to probe the effects of regional involvement in his fiction. While it is a very different novel from those we have looked at so far, there is evident in *Farewell*—as throughout the Chandler canon—the overriding Southland theme of dissolution. It is evident, in fact, on at least three interpretive strata.

There is, first, the dream destroyed. The novel's plot from the opening page on draws its impetus from Moose Malloy's dream of reunion with his lost love, Velma Valento. Admittedly, it is a dream rooted in the sleazy world of gangsters, two-bit nightclubs, and third-rate entertainers; it is the dream of a corrupted dreamer (a theme we have seen repeatedly), a ruthless thief and murderer; and its object is a deceitful woman. But it is a dream nonetheless, and (like Cain's treatment of Cora's dream) even sentimentalized by Chandler. Such dreams, of course—like the dreams of salvation amidst the citrus, sunshine, and celebrities dreamt by West's locusts—must fail in the end. As it turns out, this dream dies only moments before the dreamer himself does, with five bullets shot into him by the very object of his dream.

At another level, *Farewell, My Lovely* is a narrative of the breakdown of human society and its major nesting place, the contemporary city. The Los Angeles that Philip Marlowe traverses is, across its massive breadth and along its entire sociological spectrum, a physically and morally decayed conurbation set mockingly in the splendid but ever-threatening natural landscape at the end of the American West.

And along with Hammett and the other *Black Mask* writers of the twenties and thirties, Chandler breaks from the century-old conventions of the detective story itself, the Dupin-Holmes school of aloof, unemotional, and supremely intellectual detective protagonists who, by solving a single crime and bringing to justice a single offender, restore the moral equilibrium and innocence temporarily lost within a closed milieu. This is "not that kind of story," says Marlowe, "not lithe and clever. . . . just dark and full of blood." As Chandler sees it, his fiction takes "murder away from the upper classes, the weekend house party and the vicar's rose garden, and [gives it] back to the people who are really good at it." [3] It is fiction in which suspense and ratiocination are only "the olive in the Martini," fiction played against a sordid milieu from which events cannot be dissociated. Though no oaf, Chandler's Marlowe is more brawny than brainy ("You have a lovely build, mister," Helen Grayle tells him repeatedly). He is a private detective who cracks a mystery not with Olympian intellect but through hunches, trial and error. He is a vulnerable hero who takes his lumps, and he knows fear. In Marlowe's world, innocence does not exist at the beginning; hence there is none to restore.

Farewell, My Lovely develops many of the same patterns of dissolution evident in other Southland novels. As detective fiction, it quite naturally inclines toward certain of them as major motifs—particularly questions of identity and the inadequacy of constituted authority. As fiction of the hard-boiled, antiheroic mode, it turns that inadequacy into blatant corruption, and it makes of violence as pervasive a factor as it is in Cain, McCoy, or West.

The plot turns on the question of Helen Grayle's identity, her reemergence as the beautiful blonde wife of an influential millionaire after a less auspicious start as Velma Valento, a gangster's moll. Chandler leads us on a generically typical goose chase for identity by planting amidst Jessie Florian's yellowed belongings, there to be found by Marlowe, a false photograph of Velma, a photo of a girl with reddish hair and a commonly pretty face who looks more like the ubiquitous Anne Riordan than Helen Grayle. Velma's ultimate capture and suicide occur when a detective penetrates yet another of her identities, that of "a handsome black-haired, black-browed torcher" in a Baltimore nightclub. (The "black" identity turns out to be her "true" one.) The novel's plot-impelling murder takes place against a background of elusive identity: Florian's, where Moose Malloy hunts for Velma and slaughters Sam Montgomery, has gone from white to black, still bearing the sign of its previous white owner, Mike Florian. Questions of identity also surround the two Bay City detectives, Galbraith and Blane. We are made to puzzle over who they are and what their relationship is to Jules Amthor, at whose hilltop villa we first encounter them.

In a crime report overheard on police radio, the suspect who is identified by eye-witnesses as "a middle-aged man wearing a dark grey suit and grey felt hat," turns out to be "a fourteen-year-old Mexican armed with a water pistol." Even the novel's most easily identifiable character, Moose Malloy, repeatedly thought to be cornered by police is misidentified; the captive always proves to be someone else.

The pervasiveness of violence in Chandler's world is sufficiently established by the novel's five murders, to which are added a numerous (almost comic) succession of "sappings," beatings, and violent threats, and a gruesome spreading about of victims' brains (as lusty symbol for the breakdown of reason in this violent milieu). Chandler makes clear, no less than West, how endemic this violence is. At one point, we see Lieutenant Randall casually kill two black widow spiders outside Jessie Florian's house (slaughtered widows foreshadowing the slaughtered widow inside). The lethargic desk clerk at the Hotel Sans Souci brags how quiet a place the murdered Sam Montgomery had been running: "Ain't nobody been knifed there in a month." Even Marlowe's own impulse to violence demands expression. Encountering Red Norgaard on the dock, Marlowe tells us, "He had three inches on me and thirty pounds. But it was getting to be time for me to put my fist into somebody's teeth even if all I got for it was a wooden arm." [4]

Perhaps the most obvious of all disintegrations in Chandler's Los Angeles—one wholly consistent in Southland fiction—is the breakdown of constituted authority. As the British critic John Whitley points out, the traditional formula for detective fiction puts the police at the periphery of the action (both the physical and the cerebrative action), there to await solutions from the protagonist *extraordinaire*, a private sleuth. Chandler alters the formula, making his protagonist (in Whitley's words) "a middleman caught between the police and his clients, *both* of whom may be crooked and try to kill him." [5] At their worst, as in Bay City, the police are not only corrupt but murderous, from the chief on down. Olson, their man on pickpocket detail, will "once in a while . . . lift a leather and plant it, to keep up his arrest record." Bay City's one good cop, Red Norgaard, has been thrown off the force. When questioned by Marlowe, detective Galbraith insists that police corruption is self-perpetuating. "Cops don't go crooked for money," he says. "They get caught in the system. . . . A guy can't stay honest if he wants to. . . . You gotta play the game dirty or you don't eat." The business of police work at Los Angeles's 77th Street Division, a cut above Bay City's, transpires in "a bare room with two small desks against opposite walls and room to move between them, if two people didn't try at once. Dirty brown linoleum covered the floor and the smell of old cigar butts hung in the air." Lieutenant Nulty, short-tempered, shirt frayed, is unimaginative and helpless without Marlowe's hunches and Marlowe to pursue them. Beyond Nulty's own shortcomings, the department refuses to provide resources for solving just "another shine killing." Even at the novel's periphery do we see numerous images of police indifference or helplessness. Outside the station house, Marlowe spots "two prowl-car men . . . scowling at a bent front fender." After a lengthy talk with Nulty inside, he comes out and sees "the prowl-car men . . . still looking at their bent fender." When the wooden-faced chauffeur driving Marlowe to Amthor's illegally makes a U-turn, "a cop across the street said: 'Hey,' weakly, as if he didn't mean it, and then bent down quickly to tie his shoe." Lieutenant Randall's two beefy assistants stand behind him spitting and looking suspicious at every cue. Even Randall, the novel's only competent cop, with all the "smartness and deadliness" Marlowe attributes to him, is "not free to do a clean job in a clean way." At one point, Randall himself blurts out, "Police work. Phooey." Further symbolizing the impotence of legal authority, Laird Brunette's off-shore gambling ships loom on the ocean horizon. "We're not in Bay City now," the tough young greeter on the *Montecito* tells Marlowe, "not even in California, and by some good opinions not even in the U.S.A. Beat it."

Other forms of dissolution are evident too. All trace of innocence has disappeared in Chandler's characters. Marlowe may be effectively "celibate," as both Whitley and

Philip Durham call him,[6] but his is not self-sacrificing celibacy. It is an abstinence symbolizing the breakdown of love in Chandler's Southland. Chandler felt that the "peculiar appropriateness of the detective or mystery story to our time is that it is incapable of love. The love story and the detective story cannot exist," he said, "not only in the same book—one might almost say in the same culture. Modern outspokenness has utterly destroyed the romantic dream on which love feeds." [7] Even Anne Riordan who, once absolved of our suspicions, comes as close to a symbol of feminine purity and loyalty as we get in the novel, is more modernly outspoken than innocent, extremely forward in forcing Marlowe's attentions upon her, and by no means reluctant to express her affection for him.

Love's demise is signaled in the novel's opening paragraph as we learn that a deserted Mrs. Aleidis is "willing to spend *a little* money" to find her husband [italics mine]. Jessie Florian hates her late husband Mike. Velma tramples on Moose Malloy's love and, as Helen Grayle, disdains her husband's. "Who was that?" she asks Marlowe as their embrace is interrupted. "Mr. Grayle," he tells her. "Forget him," she says. The young "lovers" who ride with Marlowe on the launch out to the *Montecito* "chew each other's faces," and when the launch arrives take their "teeth out of each other's necks . . . and giggle."

Dreams also die: not only Moose's dream, but Velma's too—a desire for respectability so strong that it leads her to self-protective murder. On our way to Lindsay Marriott's murder in Purissima Canyon, we see "a broad avenue lined with unfinished electroliers and weed-grown sidewalks [where] some realtor's dream had turned into a hangover." Traditional values again break down. Mrs. Morrison, Jessie's busybody neighbor, voices the modern American complaint: "Folks ain't safe a minute in this town. When I come here twenty-two years ago we didn't lock our doors hardly. . . ." Marlowe recognizes his own separation from traditional values. "I needed a lot of life insurance," he tells us. "I needed a vacation, I needed a home in the country. What I had was a coat, a hat and a gun." On the malodorous beach front, where in quieter times a picturesque streetcar used to turn, "now a big blue bus blared" in dissonant plosives down the strand.

Pervasive, too, is the dissolution of human relationships. The key to Marriott's murder proves to be Helen Grayle's distrust and fear that he would reveal her former identity. Chandler generalizes this breakdown—as do his fellow Southland writers—by, among other things, exploiting ethnic prejudice. Like Madge Allen in *Postman*, Marlowe alludes condescendingly to Mexican bellhops. The novel's first danger sign is the transitional neighborhood described in its opening sentence: "one of the mixed blocks over on Central Avenue, the blocks that are not yet all negro." The murder of Negroes is ignored by police and press as not worth the trouble. Lieutenant Nulty tells Marlowe of the time

> "five smokes carved Harlem sunsets on each other down on East Eighty-four. . . . There was blood on the furniture, blood on the walls, blood even on the ceiling. I go down and outside the house a guy that works on the *Chronicle*, a newshawk, is coming off the porch and getting into his car. He makes a face at us and says, 'aw, hell, shines,' and gets in his heap and goes away. Don't even go in the house."

Chandler's characters tend—as they do typically in the region's fiction—to be rootless and wandering. Velma Valento is only the most obvious example of a personal break with the past. Jessie Florian is monstrously alone. Mrs. Morrison laments the nice home in Iowa "we had . . . once, me and George." Though Chandler would years later, in "The Simple Art of Murder," fill in the past of Philip Marlowe, here Marlowe is a loner whose roots are wholly unalluded to. He lives alone in an apartment with a "homely smell, a smell of dust and tobacco smoke, the smell of a world where men live, and keep living." He is alone on the job too, no sidekick, no secretary.

And there are intimations in *Farewell* of still other forms of familiar Southland dissolution: a breakdown of clear-cut sexual distinction in Lindsay Marriott, "a lad . . . [with] a thick, soft brown neck, like the neck of a strong woman," and distinctly feminine affectations; a reduction of human physical characteristics to animal likeness—Moose Malloy's, the Negro bouncer's, the Indian Second Planting's. There is even an attempt to corrupt the fundamentals of human biology—"Get hungry, folks. Get hungry," yells the voice of a concessionaire on the oceanfront. We see the same breakdown of language in characters' frequent recourse to cliché, characters like Nulty and Mrs. Morrison, and Detective Galbraith who so often monosyllabically repeats himself that Marlowe dubs him "Hemingway." We see, too, the breakdown of another of man's more humanizing impulses, that toward sentimentality (which demise is the major implication of the "hard-boiled" rubric). At the end, Marlowe wants to view Helen Grayle's suicide as good fortune for her husband, who would thereby be spared the court trial of a woman he "had loved not wisely, but too well." But Randall chides him, "That's just sentimental." To which Marlowe defers. And we see again—though the narrative never goes near the corruptive influence of a movie studio— the breakdown of art. Art is dead, explicitly, in the ridiculous architectural trappings of the Grayle mansion: crouching griffins in the garden, stone water lillies and bullfrogs in an oblong pool, a wrought-iron gate with a flying Cupid in the middle (mocking the lovelessness within); and it is dead by implication in the smeary reproduction of Rembrandt's self-portrait hanging in Marlowe's office. What again ascends in art's place is an unabashed profit motive. Rembrandt's "other hand held a brush poised in the air, as if he might be going to do a little work after a while, if somebody made a down payment." The aging Rembrandt is Marlowe's alter ego; Marlowe himself, though dubious of Marriott and the job he offers, chooses nonetheless to accompany him to Purissima Canyon—for the hundred-dollar fee. Chandler would later, as a screenwriter, decry Hollywood's rape of artistry and call money the place's "all pervasive agent." [8] Clearly, though, the breakdown of art and the concomitant thriving of the fast-buck impulse were a part of his Los Angeles vision before his work as a scenarist.

While violence dominates the novel, other of the Southland's supportive motifs are clearly in evidence. Throughout Chandler and the new detective genre one witnesses the same kinetic speed-up. From any logical standpoint the novel's narrative pace is impossibly swift. Its events speed by in an incredibly tight hour-by-hour schedule. Marlowe meets Malloy; Malloy murders Sam Montgomery; Marlowe is questioned by Nulty, pays a visit to the desk clerk at the Sans Souci, tracks down Jessie Florian, gets a call from Lindsay Marriott, and goes to Marriott's home; they ride to Purissima Canyon and Marriott is murdered there; Marlowe stumbles upon Anne Riordan in the hills, returns to the city with her, is questioned by Randall, then after daybreak is reconfronted by Anne; and after she leaves he finds Amthor's business card, calls Amthor, and finally has his flash of insight into the link between Marriott and Jessie Florian—all during the narrative's first twenty-four hours. Even during lulls in the action, such as they are, Marlowe is aware—like Jim Malloy in *Hope of Heaven*—of constant sound and motion, the incessant bonging of the traffic light and the movement of traffic beneath his window.

Helping to shape Chandler's narrative are also numerous regionally consistent images of façade, falseness, and artificiality. Beneath every posh or picturesque veneer, things are hollow, shabby, sleazy. The phonily architected Grayle mansion is guarded over by an ersatz young cossack. Lindsay Marriott's house displays "an imitation coach-lamp" and "a knocker in the shape of a tiger's head." Behind the neon sign of Florian's, and its "swing doors [which] closed off . . . whatever was beyond," we see a coffinlike "long narrow room." The Bay City vista outside Chief Max's window— "the busy bustle of Arguello Boulevard and the lovely California foothills . . . one of the nicest little business sections a man could want to know. . . . the finest yacht harbor [etc.]"—is one of the novel's most obvious examples of a placid façade masking a foul and corrupt interior. The outside of Dr. Sonderborg's sanatorium too—"like the home of an elderly well-to-do couple who like to garden"—is a deceptive front behind which transpires the evil emblematic of Chandler's city.

The novel's plot revolves, of course, about a cleverly

played role by Velma Valento, a role whose falseness ob-
trudes when, as Helen Grayle, she dispenses with social
amenity and says to Marlowe: "To hell with this polite
drinking. . . . Let's get together on this." Lindsay Marriott
works hard at a role which ultimately betrays him. Minor
characters like Galbraith, Amthor, and Second Planting are
all poseurs. Even in fleeting imagery does the role-playing
motif recur. The men with "sharp foxy faces and racetrack
clothes or eccentric clown-like make-up" in Jessie Florian's
"shiny photographs of men and women in professional
poses" distinctly recall West's masqueraders on Vine Street,
O'Hara's Red Luck, and the garish roles that McCoy's
marathoners were called upon to play.

Reality blurs into illusion not only with the novel's many
erroneous "eye-witness" reports, but with the sailors and
their girls at the beach front "having their photos taken
riding on camels," and the launch pilot's careening the boat
around in curves to simulate "thrills." Marlowe himself, at
several points, cannot distinguish reality from illusion. He
awakens in the sanatorium with thin lines of "smoke" before
his eyes, and escapes the room in one of the novel's tensest
moments "yawning a great deal." The entire narrative is
played against the Southland "unreality" of hot weather in
March.

Two-dimensional characterizations pervade the novel: the
brutish and apelike Moose Malloy, the "rich-bitch" Helen
Grayle, the eager and ubiquitous Anne Riordan, and a collection of stereotyped cops and Negroes. As part of a regional
fiction which seems to encourage polarities of character type,
Marlowe is a quintessential initiate in an environment where
uninitiates are doomed. But as Whitley points out, he is an
initiate with remnants of knightly virtue, with an unfulfilled
longing for the other extreme, a bygone innocence.[9]

The novel's tone—heavy with the fatalistic irony of its
author's own cynical moralism—also ties it close to the
Southland corpus. Marlowe's habitual metaphor is the ironic
simile. Moose Malloy on Central Avenue is "as inconspicuous
as a tarantula on a slice of angel food"; he is a big man, "but
not more than six feet five inches tall and not wider than a

beer truck!" Chief Max is as "polite as a bouncer at the Stork Club." The frayed lamps at Jessie Florian's are "as gay as superannuated street-walkers." The Grayle mansion is really "not so much. It was smaller than Buckingham Palace, and probably had fewer windows than the Chrysler Building." Getting slowly out of bed the morning after his escape from Sonderborg's, Marlowe is sick, but "not as sick as I would feel if I had a salaried job." The novel also abounds with ironic tag names: Mrs. Grayle (Moose Malloy's grail, and in a different way Marlowe's); Dr. Amthor (*am Thor*, a self-proclaimed phony God figure); the rusty gambling ships, *Montecito* (after one of California's most picturesque and affluent neighborhoods) and *Royal Crown* (where gambling and corruption are king). Characteristically, the novel's irony is stretched to hyperbolic proportions. Lieutenant Nulty, we are told, is the kind of guy who would make a swell brakeman on a boxcar that had no wheels. Marlowe's nourishment at the beach front is an eighty-five-cent dinner which "tasted like a discarded mail bag and was served . . . by a waiter who looked as if he would slug me for a quarter, cut my throat for six bits, and bury me at sea in a barrel of concrete for a dollar and a half, plus sales tax."

Marlowe's cynicism is explicit as he unravels the "cigarettes" from Marriott's case: "Marijuana. . . . American hashish. A weed that would grow anywhere. Unlawful to cultivate now. That meant a lot in a country as big as the U.S.A." That cynicism is also clearly implied in the face of Rembrandt, Marlowe's alter ego: a face "aging, saggy, full of the disgust of life and the thickening effects of liquor." But Rembrandt also reflects something of Marlowe's stoicism ("[that face] had a hard cheerfulness that I liked"). It is a stoic cynicism ("My head hurt . . . my throat was stiff . . . my jaw was not untender. But I had had worse mornings"), and a cynicism resigned to its own bleakly deterministic outlook ("My left foot felt fine. . . . So I had to kick the corner of the bed with it").

Though Chandler alone among the writers considered in this study was not a scenarist prior to writing his fiction, his narrative technique in his earlier (and better) Southland novels is, like the others', episodic and highly visual. When Marlowe regains consciousness in the sanatorium, we are made to experience his visual sensations. His flash of insight into the Florian-Marriott relationship—though more directly renderable in his first-person monologue—is given us through visual tableau:

> The thought hit. . . . like a dropped brick. I stopped and leaned against the marble wall and pushed my hat around on my head and suddenly I laughed.
>
> A girl passing me on the way from the elevators back to her work turned and gave me one of those looks which are supposed to make your spine feel like a run in a stocking. I waved my hand at her and went back to my office and grabbed the phone.

The character of Marlowe owes as much to visual imagery as it does to expressed points of view or self-scrutiny:

> Marriott arranged himself in the curve of the grand piano, leaned over to sniff at the yellow rose, then opened a French enamel cigarette case and lit a long brown cigarette with a gold tip. I sat down on a pink chair and hoped I wouldn't leave a mark on it. I lit a Camel, blew smoke through my nose and looked at a piece of black shiny metal on a stand.

"If you want the feel and aspect of Los Angeles and vicinity during the thirties . . ." says George P. Elliot, "you could hardly do better than to read [Chandler's] fiction." [10] "The picture and pulse of the city," says Philip Durham, "[are] so described that the reader on his first visit had a haunting feeling that he had been there before." [11] Elliot and Durham are not alone. No writer's work has been more closely associated with place than Chandler's with Los Angeles. To date, that relationship has been the nexus for most Chandler criticism. It is indeed more than a superficial one. Chandler draws broadly upon the multiplicitous city and its surroundings—from the canyons above Malibu to the Santa Monica beach front, from West Los Angeles to Hollywood Boulevard and the tawdry central city district.

The Malibu hills, which mocked the receding hopes of Gloria Beatty and Robert Syverten, are used by Chandler to suggest an ominous aloneness as Marlowe and Marriott proceed toward the fatal ransom spot: "A yellow window hung here and there, all by itself, like the last orange." Mountain canyon is again the site of brutal murder; Marriott's head is caved in not far from where Nick Papadakis's was. Marlowe himself comes nearest death at Amthor's mountain retreat. The damp salt air and ocean wind are used to foreshadow Marriott's "impermanence": on the way to Marriott's, Marlowe passes a "salt-tarnished spiral of staircase" leading up a hill, steps "drifted over with wind-blown sand," and hears the clatter of the knocker "swallowed in the early evening fog." The physical defilement of the Santa Monica oceanfront parallels the spiritual defilement of contemporary urban man: "There was a faint smell of ocean," Marlowe tells us. "Not very much, but as if they had kept this much just to remind people this had once been a clean open beach where the waves came in and creamed and the wind blew and you could smell something besides hot fat and cold sweat." The shabby urban landscape of the central city is used to anticipate certain dimensions of Jessie Florian's character. She lives in

> a dried-out brown house with a dried-out brown lawn in front of it. There was a large bare patch around a tough-looking palm tree. On the porch stood one lonely wooden rocker, and the afternoon breeze made the unpruned shoots of last year's poinsettias tap-tap against the cracked stucco wall. A line of stiff yellowish half-washed clothes jittered on a rusty wire in the side yard.

One can hardly miss the "loony sign" tapped out on behalf of the cracked old woman within.

Though *Farewell, My Lovely*, like most of Chandler's fiction, takes place on the edges of Hollywood—ignoring the industry's abundance of useful fictional materials, its actors, writers, studio sets, and manufactured illusions—the novel is still largely shaped by the aesthetic influences of region, a literary region which, though centered in Hollywood, spreads psychologically across the California Southland. Significantly, Marlowe, who moves widely across Los Angeles and the surrounding landscape, lives in Hollywood and operates out of an office at the heart of Illusionland, on Hollywood Boulevard. The novel's comments on region are aimed contemptuously at some of the same targets attacked by West, the area's occultist charlatans and its medical quacks. "Give him enough time," Marlowe says of Amthor, "and pay him enough money and he'll cure anything from a jaded husband to a grasshopper plague. . . . But mostly it would be women . . . women of all sizes, shapes and ages, but with one thing in common—money." Dr. Sonderborg's sanatorium for dope addicts is a place where, for a fee, hoods on the lam can lay low.

Beyond its quite discernible regionality, *Farewell, My Lovely* is exceptionally good mystery fiction. (At least one critic has called it a masterpiece.)[12] The book must ultimately, as its author wished, be judged within that genre. Looked at objectively, one sees it not entirely free from the weaknesses characteristic of that genre. The double role played by Velma Valento doubles her burden of credibility, and she never fully convinces us as either society lady or ex-moll. Awkward too is the novel's inordinate dependence upon coincidence—Ann Riordan's turning up (to attract our suspicions) in Purissima Canyon right after Marriott's murder; Malloy's hiding away at Dr. Sonderborg's behind a conveniently open door, Red Norgaard's appearance at the Bay City dock—all at precisely the proper moment in Marlowe's hectic schedule. One can argue, of course, as Norman Rabkin does in another context, that dramatic coincidence when hand in hand with subtle foreshadowings of an outcome is but another kind of useful aesthetic "distortion," a distortion more of convention than of reality, one which helps to create an aura of destiny about a story, a sense of inevitability about that outcome.[13] Certainly the flatness of character and the sense of kinetic speed-up we get in the novel, as throughout Southland fiction, tell us something specific about the world in which the action occurs. So too does the novel's succession of well-timed entrances reinforce our sense of a deterministic universe. But Chandler's co-incidences begin too early, are unaccompanied by any hint of the mystery's outcome, and are used unwisely on several occasions to introduce pivotal characters, like Red Norgaard, whom we never knew existed. As a result, the novel's coincidences convey less a sense of destiny than contrivance.

But fully successful or not as general fiction, Chandler's novel is among the very best of a type, engrossing us indeed as much by its malaise as by its puzzle. Certainly the novel's fortuitous twists and entrances, its hyperbolic flatness of character, its breakneck pace, its blood and its gore, give it a narrative audacity which marks the book as much a product of region as of its author's vision of the human predicament. And it shows us again how indelible that mark of region can be.

6

Tycoon Sammy

Although for the most part critically ignored (and when not, usually maligned), Budd Schulberg's first novel, *What Makes Sammy Run?* (1941), is a curiously remarkable book —remarkable for the extent of both its weaknesses and strengths. The story of its title character's meteoric rise in Hollywood, the novel is narrated by an authorial mask, Al Manheim, sometime drama critic for the New York *Record*, in a series of vignettes at successive plateaus in Sammy's ascent. Manheim first encounters Sammy Glick running copy at the *Record* and, after becoming enthralled by Sammy's incandescent gall, follows him to Hollywood, there to labor as one of a legion of minor screenwriters while Sammy claws and connives his way into the top spot at World-Wide Pictures. Manheim's fascination over Sammy is a mixture of awe and contempt, an unexceptional ambivalence, but a potentially volatile narrative posture nonetheless. Unfortunately, its author's motive shows through. As vehicle for the very youthful Schulberg's polemic against prevailing American values and social conditions, that fascination is expressed with such self-righteous commonplace that the novel is threatened by banality.

Resisting the novel's flaccid narrative, however, is Sammy himself, one of American fiction's most memorable caricatures. A brash young Jew from the Lower East Side, Sammy parlays a plagiarized script into a job as columnist, and in a few short years with relentless drive, unscrupulous opportunism, and a genius for self-promotion becomes boy wonder

of the motion picture industry. In drawing Sammy, Schulberg aims not so much for a character as a quintessence—
that of the slick operator—and he endows him with wit and
vitality sufficient to break through the novel's narrative
blandness.

From our special perspective, Schulberg's novel brings us
to regional ground-zero with its focus on the inner workings
of the movie industry. Most of the (by now) regionally
predictable elements are here, central among them the
seemingly imperative dissolution theme. Schulberg calls this
first novel an attempt "to throw some light on one of the
less glamorous but not insignificant phases of Hollywood
life." [1] As its narrative unfolds, that "not insignificant phase"
proves nothing less than the coming apart of a young but
vital American institution. The industry of Griffith, Chaplin,
and Thalberg, with its already legendary successes and its
limitless potential, is, by the late thirties, being remade into
a superficial medium of mass entertainment, newly presided
over by the wheeler-dealers and profit-mongers who have
replaced its founders, by Sammy Glick and all the newer
and fresher Sammy Glicks who will "spring up to harass
. . . threaten . . . and finally overtake" the current Sammy.

Artistry breaks down (as it does throughout the region's
fiction) and is overcome by a voracious appetite for profit.
(Taken together, Schulberg's two Hollywood novels—*Sammy*
and *The Disenchanted* [1950]—are opposite sides of this
same thematic coin. Manly Halliday, Schulberg's *roman à
clef* Fitzgerald, personifies the death of artistry, and Sammy
the ascendence of the slick operator.) Like West's Mrs.
Johnson who silences Bach "in the middle of a phrase,"
Sammy, in collusion with the "Wall Street crowd," finally
silences Sidney Fineman, forcing him out of the top spot
at World-Wide Pictures and into an early grave. Fineman
"was a picture maker" with pride in his work, a man making
classics "like *Helen of Troy* when everyone else was making
two-reel horse operas." Taking over Fineman's office, Sammy
rips out its Colonial motif ("because he said it cramped
him"), and gives it "the intimacy of Madison Square
Garden," with leather-lined walls and a "solid glass desk

. . . like a burlesque runway." Earlier on, when Sammy concocts a ridiculous "switcheroo" on Maugham's *Rain* for a third-rate producer, Kit Sargent, still in the throes of her own attraction to Sammy, warns Manheim: "As long as they sell South Seas pictures before they know what they're going to be about . . . the kind of ad libbing Sammy just gave us will be a work of genius." The novel's clearest emblem of the death of art in Hollywood is its resident poet, Henry Powell Turner. A Pulitzer Prize winner, once handsome and statuesque, this Turner has turned, after several years in Hollywood, into a vulgar and drooling alcoholic living with an unfaithful wife in "the largest example of the worst kind of architecture" Manheim has ever seen. The mansion that later marks Sammy's accession is a conglomerate "Persian-Spanish-Baroque-Norman, with some of the architect's own ideas thrown in to give it variety." What Sammy's rise means to art in Hollywood is clear in a chat he and Manheim have about Ignazio Silone's *Fontamara*:

> "Who the hell is Ignats Silone?" he said.
> "For my dough one of the greatest writers in the world," I said.
> "No kidding!" He was interested. "Has he got a good story?"
> "One of the greatest stories I ever read," I said. "All about how a ragged little group of peasants rise against Mussolini."
> "Well, for Chri'sake, who do you think's gonna make a picture about a lot of starving wops? In the first place, you'd lose your whole foreign market and . . ."

Art is not the only traditional value in disintegration. Sammy's *modus operandi* is so thoroughly plagiaristic that even his curbside expletives are reissued folk cries of the New York gutters. His story-telling ability, which propels his rise, reflects the new value system in Schulberg's Hollywood.

> First, no qualms. Not the thinnest sliver of misgiving about the value of his work. . . . In the second place, he

was as uninhibited as a performing seal. He never questioned his right to monopolize conversation or his ability
to do it entertainingly. And then there was his colossal
lack of perspective. This was one of his most valuable
gifts, for perspective doesn't always pay. It can slow you
down. . . . It can make you very unhappy. I couldn't
imagine Sammy ever unhappy. Or happy either. . . . only
[his] burning impatience to be further, further on.

Status to Sammy is a plaster mold made of his feet by the
shoe salesman: Sammy "couldn't have been more flattered
if he had been asked to pose for a bronze bust."

And Sammy is no lone embodiment of a breakdown in
traditional values. He is simply the centerpiece in a decadent
setting. When word gets around, erroneously, that Sammy's
bodyguard, Sheik Dugan, is a famous gunman, Sheik is
accorded the status of "celebrity's celebrity." The biggest
attraction at the Brown Derby (where people pay for the
privilege of watching each other) is a foreign star who comes
in with husband on one arm and lover on the other, walking
between them "with a haughty pride, the way one does with
Russian wolfhounds." The milieu is such that Manheim can
call Billie Rand (for whom sleeping with men was "the
friendliest thing people can do") "the nineteen-thirty-six
version of the old-fashioned girl."

Consistent too with the Southland pattern is the loss of
past evident in each of Schulberg's major characters. Sammy's
disdain for his ghetto upbringing is expressed repeatedly in
the novel; he is contemptuous of the Lower East Side and
his parents' Yiddishness. Both Manheim and Kit, less
meanly born, have also veered from pasts of parental aspiration. Four years at Wesleyan, under Methodist auspices,
have turned Manheim away from the rabbinical calling his
father had held out for him. Kit's emancipated "bachelor-
hood" stems from her rebellion against a possessive mother.
Each is torn from his past, yet not quite at home in Hollywood's transient present. Manheim talks of "getting set" in
Hollywood, but corrects himself—"or as set as a bewildered
stranger ever gets in this town."

Yet another dimension of dissolution borne in common with other Southland fictions is the novel's breakdown of significant communication. Sammy Glick is a creature of the pun, the twisted word, and the cliché. Accused by Manheim of ethical cheapness, Sammy retorts, "Sure, it was cheap. . . . After all, I got better publicity free than you could have bought for big dough. You can't ask for anything cheaper than that." Language at meetings of the Screen Writers' Guild is misleading and deceptive: "gagging" is an "official court language" beneath which "you could feel the friction growing." At a number of points, Schulberg has Manheim parody the pervasiveness of cliché in Hollywood:

> Out of sheer desperation I asked [Sammy's secretary] if there wasn't anything else a person could be in a story conference besides tied up, but she didn't even chuckle.

> It's wonderful what a few drinks of Scotch will do on an empty brain.

> "I don't know much about art," I said, "I only know what I like. I think it stinks."

Unfortunately, even more of Manheim's clichés are unintended by Schulberg.

Finally, love, that favorite victim of the Southland writer, is once again rendered a dead issue; and sexuality (though in a way, I think, not wholly intended by Schulberg) seems curiously inverted. Before he falls for Laurette Harrington, the devil-may-care daughter of World-Wide's board chairman, Sammy thinks he might like to settle down with little Ruth Mintz. "Do you love her?" asks Manheim. "Love," Sammy says, "how the hell have I had time to love anybody?" Later married to Laurette, Sammy is cuckolded on his very wedding night. Manheim's affair with Kit and their ultimate engagement never do ring true. There is no chemistry to their relationship. Manheim's first proposal is as perfunctory as Jim Malloy's to Peggy Henderson: "Maybe I would be calling you by the time I reached Needles. So why don't you save us both a lot of time by coming with me?

We'll get married when we get in." Kit's own expressions of affection for Manheim, at their warmest, are ambivalent.

The false ring to Manheim's affair with Kit is in curious contrast to his strong and (it would seem) not wholly platonic or self-serving attraction to Sammy. Readers who question the credibility of Al's compulsive pursuit of his "little Sammy Glick" should note some of the ways that attraction is expressed and that pursuit described. As one of an amorous foursome in Sammy's apartment, Al is comfortably involved in Billie's embrace, yet he becomes agitated when Sammy slips off into the bedroom with Sally Ann: "Sinking to the couch with Billie, I remembered a similar revulsion years ago. . . ." Hung over the next morning, he spends the day, "of all places, in Sammy Glick's bed," after Sammy has gone. "When I awoke again . . . I had a bad taste in my mouth and a worse one in my mind. . . . I went straight from Sammy's to a Turkish Bath, where I abandoned myself to steam and sweat. . . ." Shortly after this episode, Al expresses his attraction to Sammy in terms of agony and penetration:

> There was no use kidding myself any longer. I wanted to know him. . . . If I broke off now, I had the feeling his memory would go on torturing me. I had the crazy feeling that only by drilling into him, deeper and deeper, could I finally pass through him and beyond him. . . .

—at which moment the phone rings and Sammy's voice, on the other end, says tauntingly "Hiya sweetheart, don't you love me anymore? . . . How's tricks at that sausage factory of yours?" Later on at a theater preview, Manheim interprets the look on Sammy's face (when his credit is flashed on the screen) as one of "deep sensual pleasure." "I felt it was something I should not be allowed to see, like the face of the boy who roomed across the hall from me in prep school when I had made the sordid mistake of entering without knocking." These intimations of homosexual attraction are by no means systematic or abundant, nor do they enter into the story's resolution. They are simply there, occasionally and suggestively, complicating Al's relationship to Sammy (as well as Schulberg's to his subject) and his mission as the novel's moral spokesman. They also echo clearly a theme familiar to Southland fiction.

Schulberg clearly does intend in the novel not merely an industry exposé, but a portrayal of the industry and its environment as an American microcosm, a place whose ethical and spiritual decomposition signals—as it does for most of Schulberg's Southland contemporaries—the death of the American Dream. Hollywood "goes to sleep at twelve o'clock," we are told, "like any decent Middle Western village." Without "the cyclamen drapes, the lush carpets, the mirrored bar, and all the rest of the trappings, . . . you would have the village beer joint." Schulberg's Hollywood centerpiece, Sammy Glick, personifies the Dream's breakdown. Belaboredly, Manheim tells us that Sammy's history is America's, "all the glory and the opportunity, the push and the speed, the grinding of gears and the crap." We are told that "Sammy intentionally and proudly glorifies the American rat"; that his double-dealing is an act in "an American tragedy"; and (in the novel's final line) that Sammy's scrapbook is "a blueprint of a way of life that was paying dividends in America in the first half of the twentieth century." At one point, Manheim can only mutter, "Sammy Glick, my Sammy Glick, my little copy boy. America, America . . . God shed His Grace on Thee and crown Thy good with. . . ." At the Vendome, Sammy "leaps to his feet like a Boy Scout at the sound of the Star-Spangled Banner" —when Louella Parsons walks in. Finally assuming control at World-Wide makes him "feel kinda . . . patriotic." The story of Sammy Glick is, in short, an Horatio Alger tale, but an Alger tale told in a decadent time with a corrupted hero. As Manheim says of Sammy's first bold steps up the Hollywood ladder, "it was Horatio Alger, it was true."

In the physical sense, Schulberg's novel avoids the violence of most Southland fiction. It is sublimated into more civilized patterns of coercion and intimidation. Other regionally related motifs, however, are undisguised. Constant speed and motion and a sense of kinetic speed-up dominate the novel —and not entirely in the person of Sammy whom Manheim likens to a "sweaty marathoner." Sammy puts "every waking moment to use" like "the famous director who even had his secretary . . . reading scripts to him through the bathroom door." Even so fundamental a process as physical maturation is, for Sammy, accelerated. It is "his own special brand, Sammyglick maturity."

> No mellowing, no deepening of understanding. . . . [just] a quickening and a strengthening of the rhythm of be-havior that was beginning to disconcert everybody who came in contact with it. Because he seemed to escape all of the doubts, the pimpled sensitivity, the introspection, the mental and physical growing pains of adolescence, he was able to throw off his youth and take on the armor of young manhood with the quick-changing ease of a chorus girl.

Manheim's office, like Jim Malloy's and Philip Marlowe's, is assaulted by continuous sound from across the way. At Ocean Park Pier, where Kit and Manheim seek refuge from the vulgar extravagance of Sammy's wedding, there is con-stant movement through dance-hall doors, an incessant churning of barrel passageways, electric shocks, trap doors in the dark, and constant motion of the ferris wheel, merry-go-round, revolving airplanes, and a roller coaster (which Kit insists on riding seven times). For the big boys in Hollywood, even sleep is "as restful as a Vorkapich Montage."

This kinetic speed-up breeds the concomitant superficiality of character we have seen before. Early on, Manheim lectures us on the difference between movie characters and "real" people:

> I suppose it's too bad that people can't be a little more consistent. But if they were, maybe they would stop being people. They might become characters in epic tragedies or Hollywood movies. Most of our characters on the screen are sandwich men for different moral attitudes. We will have the young man who stands for Honest Government and Public Service while his brother is a low-down Wal-lower in Wine, Women and Corruption.

But Schulberg's characters themselves—save for the vitality of Sammy—are little more than the moral sandwich men he blames on Hollywood. Al Manheim is everybody's Regular Guy, a man of minor talents and minor vices, ever ready to stand in judgment of the world around him. Kit Sargent is, as Chester Eisinger has noted, a stereotyped liberal intellectual—sophisticated, professionally and sexually emancipated, competent, respectable, cool, tough-fibered, equally at home in a cocktail-lounge, at work, or in bed.[2] Sammy himself is a captivating stereotype—admittedly "an unusual model. . . . with a special hopped-up motor. But . . . put out by the same people." Likie Harry Greener's face which became incapable of nuance, Sammy's begins "to settle into a permanent sneer." And like the laugh of Abe Kusich, the song of Sammy Glick is really "one note over and over again"—"Mi, mi, mi, mi . . ." Having adjusted, like Tod Hackett, to the Hollywood milieu, Kit can tell Manheim that a "little bit of Sammy would be a good thing in all of us"—much as Tod advises Homer to take a lesson in survival from the one-note dwarf.

Two-dimensional characterization leads in Schulberg as elsewhere to dichotomies of character type. To Sammy, there are only two kinds of people: those who have wised up, and suckers. The sharp distinction between insider and outsider in Hollywood comes through as clearly in Schulberg as in O'Hara. When the lunch check arrives, Manheim reaches for his wallet "but the waiter had already handed Sammy a pencil and he signed it." The distinction is even clearer between Sammy and Julian Blumberg, Sammy's hapless ghost writer. We come to learn "how many Julian Blumbergs there were, who found nothing but No Admittance signs, for every Sammy Glick who opens the lock with a wave of his cigar. . . ."

Also urged by region is the novel's juxtaposing of reality and illusion. Sammy's conception of pictures simply ignores the distinction. "I've got plenty of ideas," he tells Manheim. "One of them is to make a newspaper picture—only not the usual drunken reporter and madcap heiress crap. The real thing—the way you and I know it. Hoked up of course."

Sammy nervously awaits a first-night review, after having assured its rave by buying a full-page ad. Like West, but less effectively, Schulberg brings the unreality of the sound stage into play. Kit and Manheim, after learning of Sammy's sabotage of the fledging Screen Writers' Guild, walk down a "New York street . . . up through the Latin Quarter of Paris" and come "to a South Sea Island with . . . a native hut [and] . . . a palm tree supported with piano wire. . . ." From beginning to end—from young Sammy's brazen long-distance call to Myron Selznick, to his climactic wedding, with Laurette's white gown belying both her past and her intentions and "the funeral rhythm of the wedding march add[ing] to the unreality of the spectacle"—reality and illusion constantly vie.

Corollary motifs of role-playing, image, and façade also mark the novel. Sammy's whole life is an ongoing role of glib self-assuredness masking a deep-seated insecurity. He is "a sucker for shoes," psychological insurance against ever needing them again. Very early in Hollywood, Sammy learns to promote his "work-in-progress" by boasting of its brilliance and pretending with melodramatic fervor that he assumes his bosses assume each new story will be a stroke of genius. Sammy withholds his highest esteem, not for any of the real talent in Hollywood, but for the Hollywood publicist, the molder of images. Even at the end, Laurette having left him, the embittered Sammy turns on all the lights, grits his teeth, and plays the *bon vivant*.

Albeit less developed by Schulberg than West or McCoy, an explicit disparagement of group man is also evident in *Sammy*. While to Kit the democratic Guild is the one real hope for Hollywood writers, to Sammy it is "nothing but a bunch of sheep. Throw one good scare into them," he claims, "and they'll run out of this place so fast you'll think it's on fire." It is Sammy who proves right. When he and the Committee of Five throw that scare, the Guild dissolves. Sammy's assessment of what pleases the movie-going public —an assessment which serves him well—is little different from Claude Estee's opinion of the barber in Purdue. Typical among the crowd outside Sammy's premiere are a plump young lady in slacks and a gangling scabby-kneed girl who shoved their autograph books in Kit's face. . . . Kit helplessly . . . scribbled her name. The child stared at the page, puzzled a moment, cried out feverishly, "That was nobody!" ripped the page out, crumpled and threw it away and fought her way into the middle of the next circle.

In *Sammy*, the deterministic world view that colors Southland fiction is given its most explicit treatment—and its most jejune. The title question raised early by Manheim —What makes Sammy run?—is ostensibly what impels him to follow Sammy's tracks back and forth across the country. Intellectual child of her time, Kit encourages Manheim to seek the answer in "the kind of infancy Sammy had, and whether his kindergarten teacher used to slap him, and under what conditions he learned the facts of life . . . the whole works." When Manheim, back in New York, finally goes down to the tenement district, he sees that indeed the "street is the real school," that Sammy had been born and nurtured not of his mother so much as "out of the belly of Rivington Street," on whose pavement he became "a star pupil," "born into the world [no] more selfish, ruthless and cruel than anybody else," but driven to prove himself "the fittest, the fiercest and the fastest" in the ongoing war on the "giant dung heaps" of the Lower East Side. With these newfound insights, Manheim sermonizes bartenders (". . . people, Henry, are just results. They're a process"); he sermonizes us ("Sammy's will had stiffened. It had been free for an instant at birth . . . before it began to be formed to the life-molds, the terrible hungers . . ."); and he even sermonizes Sammy ("I think you couldn't help yourself. . . . The world decided it for you"). Sammy scoffs at this ("don't give me that double-talk"), but arrives at a similar self-diagnosis: "Most of the Hebes I know drive me nuts because they always go around trying to be so goddam kind. It ain't natural." Morality for Sammy, from the beginning, has been a matter of percentages. Growing up, he avoided "sucker stuff" like assault and robbery that turn "the cops

against yer," in favor of things like ward heeling and pimping
that "have 'em with ya." His favorite clichés are Darwinian
—"when you come right down to it it's dog eat dog"—
which Manheim rejects as too simplistic for "thinking
animals," until he relives Sammy's first hours on Rivington
Street:

> The midwife did not think Shmelka would live. He
> weighed only five and a half pounds. "*Nebbish* such a
> little one," said the midwife. "Were he a little kitten we
> would drown him already." [But Mama Glickstein]
> pushed her great breasts into his mouth until he choked,
> hollered, and began to live.

Manheim's overbearing moralism blunts the narrative
irony that is common to most Southland fiction. Schulberg
is not insensitive to the almost palpably ironic atmosphere of
Hollywood, and he uses it to some effect. But his heart is
elsewhere. Committed to the role of novelist-as-outspoken-
moralist, he confines that irony to counterpoint in the
mouths and actions of his Hollywood insiders, Kit and
Sammy. He turns the novel's primary outlook (his own)
over to the outsider Manheim, and through Manheim offers
an unblushing corrective for the moral vacuum in which
Sammy runs. Manheim laments the kind of system which
"could give Sammy a reputation on the basis of one story he
hadn't written, while its real author [Julian Blumberg]
couldn't . . . get himself hired as a junior writer." But Kit,
after Julian is finally hired at a fourth of Sammy's salary,
can assure him, "if the ratio of talent to bombast is only
one to four . . . talent is coming up in the world." Manheim looks with respect and deference on Sidney Fineman's
pioneering achievements in cinematic art. Sammy, in public
memorial to Fineman, awards his widow "a gold life-pass to
all World-Wide pictures."

Much of Sammy's exuberance owes to Schulberg's feel for
the hyperbole endemic to Hollywood, a place where, as Kit
puts it, "every piddling little success becomes an excuse for
staging a triumph." She recalls the old Hollywood anecdote

about the three yes-men who are asked what they think of the preview. The first says it is without a doubt the greatest picture ever made. The second says it is absolutely colossal and stupendous. The third one is fired for shaking his head and saying, "I don't know, I only think it's great."

With only half the audacity, Sammy Glick would have been a remarkable phenomenon. His early manipulation of Julian Blumberg, had it not been true, says Manheim, would be "hopeless hyperbole." With bravura, Sammy favorably compares a story he hasn't written yet to a classic he's never read. Manheim can only stare in "awe for the magnitude of his blustering." For Kit as well, it is the prodigiousness of Sammy's drive that makes him attractive. He "does something to the air you breathe, intensifies it," she says—and admits to sleeping with him because "I had this crazy desire to know what it felt like to have all that driving ambition and frenzy and violence inside me."

The novel's plot development and narrative progress owe clearly to lessons Schulberg had learned as a Hollywood scenarist. From its opening *in medias res* at the *Record* to its conclusion at the baronial Glickfair some three hundred pages later, the novel is a highly visual and rapidly shifting sequence of vignettes at successive stages in Sammy's ascent. Like Sidney Fineman—who we see reduce twenty pages of a new writer's dialogue to a half-page of gesture and eye-play—Schulberg repeatedly depends on the visual correlative: Manheim's nightmare with every face in the crowd that of Sammy Glick, a dance-floor pan shot cataloging the Hollywood populace, the frozen instant of a celebrity news photo linking the vacuousness of starlet Rita Royce with the eager rapacity of Sammy.

Though unevenly wrought, the novel's employment of specifically regional items is substantial. Its cast of characters seemed sufficiently recognizable to Hollywood insiders to avoke a flood of *roman à clef* speculations, most insiders seeing Sammy as a composite drawn on Jerry Wald and Norman Krazna. The chain of events involving the Screen

Writers' Guild against which Sammy's story is played is also historically accurate. By 1936, the young Guild had gained sufficient strength to challenge industry executives and seek federal legislation to increase writers' control over their own material. In a counterattack, major producers repudiated their contract with the Guild and, led by Louis B. Mayer and Jack Warner, created their own studio-controlled organization called the Screen Playwrights. Mayer and Warner blacklisted Guild leaders and forced others to resign from its rolls. The Guild was crushed, only to be revived a year later when the National Labor Relations Act was declared constitutional, and an NLRB-sanctioned election recertified the Guild as the writers' legitimate bargaining agent.

Schulberg also draws upon the region's topography and climate. Rugged rimlands provide retreat from the Hollywood snake pit for Kit and Manheim, and give them perspective upon it. Kit's home in the hills is high above the frenetic glitter of the Trocadero, which it looks down upon. The secluded cove amidst "turbulent rock formations" on the beach beyond Malibu (which Kit ironically calls Glick's Lagoon) is another sanctuary from the falseness and glitter, a place where Kit and Manheim, with symbolic unsubtlety, strip in the cool night air and plunge purgatively into the cold surf. They return there to escape the tumultuous vulgarity of Sammy's wedding and seal their own decision to be wed. The illusory warmth of winter is evoked to reinforce the illusion of happiness through which Julian and Blanche frolic while behind their backs Sammy systematically exploits Julian's talent. Various Hollywood "institutions" of the thirties are also called into play: the Hays Office, emblem of an inhibitive false piety, and the Brown Derby, epitome of a decadent milieu. The Derby—whose star attractions, the cuckolded husband, his wife, and her lover, are the day's main source of gossip—is, as Kit puts it, Hollywood's version of the college chapel. Its acoustics, which make public the barest whisper, suggest the poisonous small-townness that Schulberg feels to be Hollywood's. Schulberg also employs (as we've seen) the dissolutionary potential of the Hollywood sound stage, but as though its use were obligatory, with nothing like the rich integration into narrative events of West's "Sargasso of the imagination." After the crunch on the Guild, Manheim elaborately contemplates folding his resignation form into an airplane and diving it into the studio street—making visual the professional suicide he was committing in Hollywood by not resigning the Guild (short-lived though that suicide proves to be). Later on, that same studio street—filled with pretty girls, cat-calling laborers, a weary director, a clown—gives ironic ring to Sammy's remark as he peers out over it: "Now it's mine. . . . I've got everything." Finally, much of the novel's Hollywood flavor owes to its abundant industry allusions, some well-integrated into the novel, others wholly self-serving. Kit paces the floor in the throes of composition, feeling "like Charlie Chaplin still going through the motions after he leaves that factory in Modern Times." In his ruthless pursuit of power, Sammy is twice likened by Manheim to the Phantom of the Opera. Billie Rand's seductiveness, we are told, is "about as subtle as Wallace Beery's acting." Sammy's nervous conversation in the novel's last scene seems "out of sync with the movement of his lips."

Another regional influence upon Schulberg—one might call it secondarily regional—is that of earlier Hollywood fiction, most notably West's. We have already noted echoes of Tod Hackett in Kit, and of Harry Greener and Abe Kusich in Sammy. The imprint of Abe Kusich (and his real-life counterpart at Hollywood and Wilcox) is also obvious on Schulberg's Hollywood photographer, a feverish dwarf named Katz who, like Abe, emblemizes the spiritual stuntedness of Hollywood. His "degree of interest in you as a photographic subject had become an accurate test of your rating in the industry." Schulberg's running personification of Hollywood, Sammy Glick, is at several points described in terms similar to West's descriptions of Faye Greener. Where Faye is "like a cork . . . dancing over the same waves that sank iron ships," spinning "gaily away" from dangerous wave after wave, Sammy "slips through and over waves like a porpoise," while other guys "with more ability than push" are "sucked in by one wave and hurled out by the next." While Faye's "originality" amounts to her selecting from the pack of predigested stories in her mind, Sammy, whose "mind drew a blank when it came to originality," would "lift ready-made situations from the shelves in the back of his mind, dust them off and insert them . . . like standard automobile parts." At one point, Manheim likens collaborative screenwriting to "rubbing two fighting cocks together." Breaking down after Laurette's infidelity, Sammy cries in "tight, strained, hysterical little sobs," sobs distinctly recalling Homer Simpson's cry "like an axe chopping pine, a heavy, hollow, chunking noise" after his discovery of Faye's equally blatant betrayal.

Schulberg's novel, by his own admission, is written primarily in judgment—and condemnation—of place. His Hollywood—that of the son of a leading film producer—is, as Kit says, a "place full of fear." It is a town where "most of us are ready to greet our worst enemies like long lost brothers if we think they can show us a good time . . . or do us any good," a place where Sammy Glick, "believe it or not," is one of the less obvious phonies. It is the Gold Rush reincarnate, "probably the only other set-up where so many people could hit the jackpot and the skids this close together." Schulberg's Hollywood, like West's, is a glittering temptress drawing people in upon its light. Sammy attracts a wide variety of hangers-on and fascinated onlookers (including Kit and Manheim), just as Faye Greener attracts men around her in that ever-tightening circle. The only fear that Sammy finally expresses is fear of all the ambitious young men who will be drawn around Laurette "like flies."

Though Manheim's sentimental self-righteousness might be excused as youthful affectation on Schulberg's part, there remain the admixture of his contempt and fascination for Hollywood, and his libidinal tug toward Sammy, to make him a hopelessly ineffectual moral spokesman. As Eisinger points out, Manheim derides motion pictures that fall into Hollywood's Golden Rut, yet he yearns to make good there.[3] He is wistful over Hollywood's great unfulfilled promise, while lured there himself by big money and sex. In human terms, such ambivalence is understandable, but it clashes with the novel's obviously moral intent and weakens it severely. In the end, Manheim's overwhelming question — What makes Sammy run? — proves only an excuse for some clichéd sociologizing, and a rhetorical hook. Certainly it is far less vital than the runner himself. Sammy Glick, a witty and audacious caricature of the hidden side of Horatio Alger, transcends the book's framework and unashamedly enters the lexicon of literary antiheroes. Unfortunately, Manheim gets revenge upon Sammy for all the indignities. His flaccid narrative imposes a critical fate upon the novel undeserved by its title character.

7

The Hero and the Hack

Had the accumulated burdens of creative frustration, alcohol, emotional strain, and an empty bank account not proved too heavy for his heart, it is possible that the years 1937 through 1940, Scott Fitzgerald's years in Hollywood, would have been the seedtime for that "later period" Edmund Wilson told him everyone was expecting from him. Fitzgerald's death, however, four days before Christmas, 1940 (and a day before West's on the highway at El Centro), gives those years and the fiction they produced the cast of finality. They are the last years spent in a Hollywood which neither honored nor was honored by him. They are the terminal phase, begun by the lure of a lucrative screenwriting contract to a debt-ridden artist at creative nadir, and sustained by the lack of anywhere else to turn. But those burdens had not deprived Fitzgerald of his powers of observation or his creative intuition – dulled them perhaps, that is a matter for reasonable disagreement, but not destroyed them. Those powers, such as they were, were turned upon the milieu he encountered, resulting in the two final sustained works of fiction we have from Fitzgerald, one born purely of his need to remain solvent (his contract had expired by 1939 and he was free-lancing), and the other out of his conception of a genuinely tragic Hollywood hero. Together, the two works, *The Pat Hobby Stories* and the uncompleted but imposing *Last Tycoon*, form a complementary pair of Hollywood perspectives, one comic, one tragic. Certainly, the *Stories* are an ephemeral achievement. *Tycoon*, in spite of its acclaim, remains too far from completion for definitive judgment. Both, however, are thoroughly regional in their fabric, and both are critically illuminated by a regional approach.

Fitzgerald wrote the seventeen Pat Hobby stories for monthly publication in *Esquire*. They appeared in the seventeen consecutive editions from January 1940 (the edition for Christmas 1939) through May 1941 (some months after Fitzgerald's death). Though the stories at the start were separately conceived, Fitzgerald did, after writing the first three, come to see them as integral parts of a larger entity. Besides numerous eleventh-hour revisions, he repeatedly reconsidered their order of appearance and became increasingly concerned over the month-by-month development of his comic protagonist and the stories' cumulative comic effect. Pat is a hack screenwriter, once in the money but now reduced to occasional and relatively low-paying jobs, and a life of boorish opportunism. He is a schemer and a bungler. He is also for Fitzgerald an exercise in self-mockery, and an emblem of the Hollywood milieu. "Pat out of Hollywood doesn't jell," said Fitzgerald.[1] In one of the best of Pat's stories, a lady artist paints a naked portrait of Pat and calls it "Hollywood and Vine."

While grinding out his monthly Pat Hobby submissions to *Esquire*, Fitzgerald was giving artistic priority—and the last of his real talent—to his own Hollywood novel. Though acclaiming West's *Day of the Locust* and reservedly praising Schulberg's *Sammy* (which he read in draft), Fitzgerald went to his grave convinced that *The Last Tycoon* would, aesthetically if not popularly, be the definitive Hollywood novel.

Looking jointly at *Pat Hobby* and *Last Tycoon* is to see (even more than in the latter alone where it is explicit) the deep impress upon Fitzgerald of the dissolution theme. To the novel, Fitzgerald was bringing not only *Gatsby*'s succinctness but its central idea, that idea which in one way or another marked virtually every Southland novel of the period, the death of the Great American Dream. In Hollywood— which he called a "dump," a "hideous town . . . full of human spirit at a new low of debasement"—Fitzgerald had found a setting more glitteringly unreal than East Egg and, in Irving Thalberg, the model for a substantively tragic hero, a model whose successes, bitter struggles, and untimely death symbolized the death of both art and individualism in America. What prevails in Fitzgerald's Hollywood is the Glick-impelled, grind-'em-out, profit-only approach of Monroe Stahr's antagonist Pat Brady (Thalberg's rival Louis B. Mayer) and the countervailing power of battalions of collectivized screenwriters and studio workers. Ignominiously, Stahr's own talents and values are corrupted before his death. In the novel's unfinished portion, Stahr was to become little better than a high-powered Pat Hobby—paranoid, scheming, unproductive, and reduced to the stature of those who ultimately break and destroy him. Stahr lacks even Pat Hobby's persistent willingness to engage in the jungle struggle for survival. Stahr dies, while Pat, and the sham and dishonesty he represents, endure. Pat's collapse of personal fortunes, *fait accompli* as we meet him, is alluded to repeatedly in the stories and capsuled by the titles in his two-volume library: the *Motion Picture Almanac of 1928* and *Barton's Track Guide, 1939*. It is testament to the omnipresence of the dissolution motif that Fitzgerald, in one of the stories' most glaring weaknesses, imposes it upon Pat without providing a trace of evidence that Pat was ever capable of those earlier successes. His professional comedown is pure *donnée*.

Both books quite clearly suggest that Hollywood's fate is America's. Both Celia Brady, whose perceptions govern the novel's narrative, and Pat Hobby, like millions of Americans, have had their mentalities shaped by motion pictures. Celia's values, her world view, her most fervent fantasies have all been conditioned by screen romance. Pat, we learn, spent his "young and impressionable years" looking through the peep-hole of the movie industry precursor, "a machine where two dozen postcards clapped before his eyes in sequence." One of Pat's most forceful studio bosses, Dick Dale, is "a type that, fifty years ago, could be found in any American town."

As James E. Miller has shown, the American past is symbolically debased at a number of points in *Last Tycoon*: most strikingly in its grotesque contrast between the spirit of Andrew Jackson and the pathetic reality of Manny Schwartz at the Hermitage, and in its tableau of Lincoln in the studio commissary, his shoulders wrapped in a shawl against the chill, hovered over by a real-life Fascist prince, stuffing a wedge of pie into his mouth.[2] This mock-Lincolnian image still lingering, Stahr himself is compared to Lincoln, "a leader carrying on a long war on many fronts." Fitzgerald's conception of the quintessential American character, unburdened by history and equipped "for aerial adventure,"[3] is made manifest in the novel's structurally embracing images of aerial flight—opening westwardly, and closing (in the unfinished section) with Stahr's fatal eastward flight of escape.

Virtually every dimension of dissolution evident in the novels we have looked at earlier assumes a role in Fitzgerald's Hollywood fiction: the loss or confusion of identity; the end of love and of innocence; the corruption of normal sexuality; human decay; the death of art, of values, and of dreams; the breakdown of language; an all-pervading sense of the waste of human energies—all are present.

In *The Last Tycoon*, confused identities reinforce our sense of Southland anonymity and severed roots. Stahr first appears under the traveling alias "Mr. Smith." The girl he takes to be Kathleen is actually her friend, one Edna Smith. The pawn in Brady's retribution against Stahr is yet another Smith, Kathleen's husband, W. Bronson Smith. Brady himself is more a symbol of depersonalized corporate power than a clearly drawn character. He never confronts us or Stahr directly. Even his daughter Celia can ask: "What did father look like? I couldn't describe him. . . ." Before his suicide, the face of Manny Schwartz, the Hollywood has-been, falls into "disintegrated alignments." Wylie White tells Celia how he ran "like a crazy man" from his first Hollywood party, feeling he had no "rightful identity." The caller on the other end of the line whom Stahr believes to be the President is really an orangoutang. While "most writers look like writers whether they want to or not, . . . Pat Hobby was the exception. He did not." His boss Mr. Banizon sends Pat on a mission to learn a plot ending from its recalcitrant creator, an ending which affects a character as yet without identity: how does the artillery shell get "in the trunk of Claudette Colbert or Betty Field or whoever we decide to use?" *The Pat Hobby Stories* also have their Smith, Priscilla, one of the many faceless young things who enter and exit Pat's life indistinguishably—giving us four unrelated Smiths as anonymity symbols in these two books.

Each of the naïve young things in this faceless parade quickly loses that naïveté. Each has her eyes opened within a very few pages. In *Tycoon*, Wylie White's earlier innocence has given way to a seasoned cynicism, as has Celia's. "I knew what you were supposed to think about [Hollywood]," she tells us, "but I was obstinately unhorrified."

Consistent too is the breakdown of love in Fitzgerald's Hollywood. Pat's three divorces and Stahr's painful widowerhood set the tone. Kathleen's engagement is no obstacle to a brief and passionate, though clearly loveless, affair with Stahr. After she marries, Stahr comes to doubt even the possibility of love. Love's instability filters down to minor characters as well. Pat's conspiratorial secretary in "Christmas Wish" is also divorced. So is Wylie White. An old liaison between Jane Maloney and John Broaca, "with whom she had had a three-day affair twenty years ago," is recalled as emotionlessly as West describes Earle's beheading of the trapped quail. Familial love fares no better. Pat is uninterested in his putative son John Indore except for the monthly allowance the boy can provide him. Before his suicide, Manny Schwartz recalls: ". . . 'Once upon a time when I was in the big money, I had a daughter,' [speaking] as if she had been sold to creditors as a tangible asset."

There are also hints in the novel—virtually gratuitous hints, but for the theme's endemic presence—of a blurring of sexual roles. Reinmund, one of Stahr's favorite supervisors, has "an almost homosexual fixation on Stahr." Broaca, who loathes Reinmund, has "never felt quite the same with himself since he . . . let Ike Franklin strike him in the face with his open hand." Sexuality dissolves with the confession of Roderiguez, the handsome matinee idol, who is hounded by women but afraid of his own marital bed. In the most revealing of Pat's stories, "Hollywood and Vine," it is the trembling Pat who is undressed by the world-weary princess.

Indeed, it is fear, not love or lust, which emotionally dominates Fitzgerald's Hollywood. "Distress in Hollywood is endemic and always acute," we learn in "Pat Hobby's Secret." Earlier, Pat is met in the studio commissary by "faces that looked at him with the universal Hollywood suspicion." Like Sammy Glick, Pat makes his way with the studio brass by stoking their fears of "Reds" in the industry—the very fear to which Monroe Stahr finally yields. Early in the novel, Wylie White makes it clear to Celia that "we don't go for strangers in Hollywood." Having learned the lesson, she later attributes her father's victory over Stahr to his having "a suspiciousness developed like a muscle."

People themselves decay prematurely in both fictions. Pat is a middle-aged lush clinging desperately to his forty-ninth birthday. At thirty-six, his secretary is "faded" and "tired," demoted from the boss's office because her presence reminded the boss of his own age. Monroe Stahr is decaying both inwardly and outwardly: his heart is bad and his legs have gone thin. Kathleen has suffered a breakdown before we meet her. Celia contracts tuberculosis. Mr. Marcus, the old producer who appears in both fictions, has the crisis-provoking heart attack in "Pat Hobby and Orson Welles," and is a basket case in *The Last Tycoon*. The pathetic Manny Schwartz represents "man" gone diminutive, and black, in Fitzgerald's Hollywood.

Quite clear as well, in both books, is the death of any impulse toward art. It is replaced, as it is throughout Southland fiction, by an unabashed profit motive. Stahr's early genius is his ability to serve both the Muse and the balance sheet. But that genius is doomed. The first hint of a reversal in Stahr's fortunes is the silence which meets his plea that the studio "make a picture that'll lose some money [and] write it off as good will." Pat, on the other hand, survives because, like Stahr's detractors, he believes "this is no art. This is an industry." Pat wins fifty dollars for thinking up the title "Grand Motel," a mockery of artistic invention. He lectures a young writer working on an adaptation on how "to get the guts out of a book." "Give the book to four of your friends to read it. Get them to tell you what stuck in their mind. Write it down and you've got a picture—see?" Pat insists to producer Jack Berners that a man can hardly be expected to have ideas when he's not on salary. Both Pat and Berners dismiss ballet as stuff for queers.

Fitzgerald's Hollywood is widely destructive of traditional values. On the novel's first page, Celia recalls the "sweet little nun" at school returning her movie script "with an air of offended surprise." Pat Hobby, of course, is a walking catalogue of corrupted values. In "A Man in the Way," he advises Priscilla Smith, reluctant to put her ideas on the open market because she's under contract, simply to "use another name." In "Christmas Wish," Pat feels his most valuable asset is a secret with which he can blackmail Harry Gooddorf. He not only deceives R. Parke Woll to learn the forgotten plot ending, but then reneges on his deal to reveal it to Mr. Banizon for fifty dollars. The epitome of corrupted value is the fact that Pat, utterly without talent or ethical worth, still commands $250 a week whenever he works, a mighty salary in Depression America.

Also marking both fictions is a regionally consistent corruption of language. Pat Hobby is incapable of speaking (or even thinking) beyond cliché. On rewrite jobs, all Pat can do is substitute one pat phrase for another. The single line he is proudest of writing is the worn-out old saw, "Boil some water—lots of it." Wylie White, a cleverer hack, quotes *Esquire* to Celia (in a burst of self-parody for Fitzgerald whose work was unwelcome elsewhere), reminding her that co-ed juniors "have nothing to learn," and that "knowledge is power." And when it isn't anemic, language in Fitzgerald's Southland is often deceptive. When Stahr asks Kathleen if she is in love with her fiancé, she replies "Oh, yes"—an " 'Oh, yes' [which] told him she was not."

We also feel in Fitzgerald, as we do in West and Schulberg, a sense of utter insignificance in the enormous energies expended to make motion pictures. Stahr inspires each of his staff "to do his part, to get his block of stone in place, even if the effort were foredoomed, the result as dull as a pyramid."

Stahr himself, for all his intense involvement in each phase of the movie-making process, "set[s] his psychological clock to run one hour," then moves on to another problem. Later in the novel, Stahr's doctor diagnoses his illness, significantly, as "a perversion of the life force."

And dreams die too. West's "Dream Dump" on the studio lot has its complement on the flickering screen of Stahr's preview room where "dreams hung in fragments at the far end of the room, suffered analysis, passed—to be dreamed in crowds, or else discarded." To Pat, the "dearest of Hollywood dreams" is, simply, "the angle."

Behind each of these many manifestations of dissolution is once again—in both books—the same panoply of secondary motifs apparently inseparable from the Southland influence: violence and death, constant sound and motion, a kinetic speed-up, crowd ugliness, a juxtaposition of reality and illusion, incongruity, pretense, disingenuousness, the playing of roles, and a pervasive two-dimensionality. Death and violence abound, openly in *Pat Hobby* and just beneath the surface in *Last Tycoon*. The *Stories* begin with attempted blackmail over apparent complicity in murder. Several stories later, Pat defends the code of the commissary hierarchy by assaulting an apparent transgressor. R. Parke Woll's death at the hands of the nightclub bouncer is as striking an emblem of senseless violence as West's mock Battle of Waterloo; it accomplishes nothing and changes nothing: Pat forgets the ending which Woll reveals to him just before his death. Manny Schwartz's suicide and the earthquake's upheaval give the novel an early backdrop of violence. In the preview room, Stahr replays the rushes of four men in a brawl: "The men fought over and over. Always the same fight." After Stahr's beating by Brimmer, the novel's unfinished portions were to focus upon labor violence, racketeering, revenge, hired murder, and a fatal plane crash.

Constant sound and motion, and a quickened sense of time pervade both fictions. Like Jim Malloy's studio, and Al Manheim's, Monroe Stahr's is never quiet: "There is always a night shift of technicians in the laboratories and dubbing rooms and people on the maintenance staff. . . . the padded hush of tires, the quiet tick of a motor running idle, the naked cry of a soprano singing into a nightbound microphone." [4] Industry people work seven days a week, around the clock, battling every new crisis in the filming schedule. Lives are more quickly expended. At forty-nine, Pat Hobby is a "venerable script-stooge." Celia and Wylie White establish their relationship in chapter one no less quickly than Robert and Gloria and Marlowe and Anne Riordan establish theirs.

Crowd-man in Hollywood fares little better at Fitzgerald's hands than he does elsewhere. The crowds at premieres "look at you with scornful reproach because you're not a star." In one of Stahr's rushes, crowds mill in worship around the head of Siva—the Hindu Destroyer.

Consistently, the most fully developed motif in Hollywood fiction—with Fitzgerald's no exception—is that of unreality, the persistent confusion between reality and illusion. Pat Hobby, a writer who doesn't look like a writer, wanders like Tod Hackett through the unreality of studio lot and sound stage. He is, at different times, caught in front of a process screen, feignedly run over by an automobile, and blown up with bogus dynamite. In "Two Old-Timers," Pat reveals the truth about an "heroic" fox-hole scene played by an effete silent-screen star whose director had to push him into the hole. The apparent murderer in "Christmas Wish" is not a murderer at all, nor the apparent commissary transgressor in "Boil Some Water" what he appears to be. An outsider in Pat's Hollywood, Sir Singrim Dak Raj, cannot mask his contempt for studio illusion. In the rushes, the flickering image of Claudette Colbert and Ronald Colman in a canoe swirling through the rapids is jarringly interrupted by Stahr's asking: "Has the tank been dismantled?" Even the pragmatic and hard-headed Pat Brady operates from a "throne room," replete with "big French windows" (of one-way glass) and a trap door (so Celia has heard) that dropped unpleasant visitors to an oubliette below. The novel's minor characters amplify this illusion motif. Martha Dodd, the washed-up actress, has delusions that her fame has only temporarily waned. The bitch actress who costs Red Ridingwood his job has eyes that photograph like starlight but, up close, a chest

and back covered with eczema. The real Jane Maloney is
hopelessly obscured behind her various images: "a sentimental dope," "the best writer on construction in Hollywood," "a veteran," "that old hack," "the cleverest plagiarist
in the biz," a nymphomaniac, a virgin, a pushover, a lesbian,
a faithful wife. In the novel's theme-setting first chapter—
which Maxwell Perkins thought "marvellously suggest[ive]" [5]
—the plane makes its descent into Hollywood going "down,
down, down, like Alice into the rabbit hole."

Much a part of the reality-illusion motif in both books
are recurrent images of incongruity. The commissary intruder
in "Boil Some Water" looks as though "someone had cray-
oned Donald Duck into the *Last Supper*." Pat's success during "the mosaic swimming-pool age [was] just before the era
when they had to have a shinbone of St. Sebastian for a
clutch lever." War's outbreak is announced in the daily
scratch sheet by a one-inch item below the form-sheets and
the past-performance listings: "LONDON, SEPTEMBER
3RD. ON THIS MORNING'S DECLARATION BY
CHAMBERLAIN, DOUGIE CABLES 'ENGLAND TO
WIN, FRANCE TO PLACE, RUSSIA TO SHOW.' "
Celia recalls a man named Dick on the back lot "standing up
in the car as if he were Cortez or Balboa, looking over [the]
grey fleecy undulation" of a lot full of sheep. The whole of
Hollywood is, as Wylie White puts it, "a mining town in
lotus land."

In Fitzgerald, as elsewhere, motifs of role-playing and disingenuousness heighten the tension between reality and illusion. Stahr's entire career, like Sammy Glick's, is a continuous starring role masking humble origins. His very body
and demeanor are extensions of the motif—princely, yet
beneath it all a bad heart and low blood pressure. Though
blessed with "extraordinary mental powers," Stahr had
"grown up dead cold" and had to learn as an adult such
things as "tolerance, kindness, forbearance, and even affection like lessons." He can dart "in and out of the role of 'one
of the boys' with dexterity"—without being one of them.
Wylie White plays the role of coequal to Stahr on the west-
ward flight, but as Celia points out it is a conventional kind

of pleasantry between top men and flunkies, an acknowledged charade. Writers in general, Celia tells us,

> aren't people exactly. Or, if they're any good, they're a whole *lot* of people trying so hard to be one person. It's like actors, who try so pathetically not to look in mirrors, who lean *back*ward trying—only to see their faces in the reflecting chandeliers.

Pat, of course, is a creature of pretense, a disingenuous phony, one of whose few moments of truth sees him running for safety back to the barroom anonymity he claims to despise when he is mistaken for Orson Welles. He is bested consistently by those who see through his phoniness, and by those like the writer René Wilcox or Princess Dignanni who are bigger phonies than he. Pat personifies the perfunctory backslap. He is quick to mouth the opinions of whomever he wishes to please. And Stahr is equally disingenuous, and much better at it. When the Tarletons, a team of Eastern playwrights, discover that he has back-up writers working on their script, they are predictably angered. The system is "a shame," Stahr admits to them, "gross, commercial, to be deplored. He had originated it—a fact that he did not mention."

Despite Fitzgerald's hopes for his tragic protagonist, there is in *Last Tycoon*—as in *The Pat Hobby Stories* and the Southland fictions of others—a pervasive flatness of characterization. For all that we see of him, Stahr remains a conventional romantic hero, the tormented genius, a hubris-ridden superman in a landscape of lesser mortals, among them a beautiful princess (Kathleen), a forsaken maiden (Celia), an evil aspirant to the throne (Brady), and a retinue of tag-named underlings, Wylie White, Red Ridingwood, Manny Schwartz, Birdy Peters. The characters in the *Stories* are an even more obvious amalgam of Hollywood stereotypes — studio bigwigs, hangers-on and flunkies, naïve young chicks, hard-boiled toughs, schemers, paranoids, prima donnas, and the rest—with not a substantially drawn character in the lot.

Tonally, as well as in theme and motif, Fitzgerald's fictions adhere to the regional patterns we have thus far discerned. Celia's narrative cynicism is only heightened by her youth.

The novel's tone is distinctly ironic, and its author's posture steadfastly moral. It is, in fact, this tonal pull toward moral irony, evident in virtually every Southland fiction, that makes *Last Tycoon* less tragic and Pat less funny than Fitzgerald hoped. With both the novel and the stories under way, he conceded to his daughter Scottie that he was "too much a moralist at heart and really want[ed] to preach at people in some acceptable form rather than to entertain them." [6] The character of Pat is developed largely through a series of ironic vignettes. He has had his heyday as a writer (i.e. a word man) in the days of silent pictures. He can lash out violently in defense of the hierarchy he is at the bottom of. For ideas, he turns to the pages of the *Times* and the *Examiner* (derided by O'Hara for their vacant provinciality). After years of stagnancy, Pat can complain: "My God! . . . How can I be expected to get anything done and show people around the lot at the same time." Several of the stories, like "A Man in the Way," are little more than singular ironies. The novel's irony is subtler, but hardly subsumed by its tragic dimension. Fearing defeat from both sides—from the corporate muscle of Brady and the collectivist fervor of Brimmer—Stahr adopts as defenses the same violent and conspiratorial qualities he fears in them, and loses to both. (Before their meeting, Stahr promises Celia that he won't hurt Brimmer.) Stahr's demise removes the last real obstacle to their ascendancy. It also, in a terminal irony planned by Fitzgerald, was to effect the comeback of a third-rate cowboy actor who, as an uninvited pallbearer, was to carry Stahr's body to the grave and consequently be deluged with new job offers.

Notwithstanding the singular grace of Fitzgerald's style, his Hollywood fictions do share the various effects upon style and narrative technique seemingly fostered by region: tendencies toward hyperbole, parody and farce; a first-person impulse; preoccupation with visual effect; and most notably the imprint of scenario writing on narrative movement. Pat Hobby is *so* much the hack that he needs a collaborator to write his dialogue, a director to take care of the gags, and someone—anyone—to supply ideas. His boss Jack Berners realizes that Pat simply cannot "write *any*thing out." After twenty years in the business, and many an oat-burner, Pat cannot even pronounce *hacienda*. He is so much the rat that he fires his secretary the day before Christmas, to save the price of a gift. "I was going to take Claudette Colbert [to the opening]," he tells an innocent young thing, "but she's got a cold. Would you like to go?" The novel, too, is peopled with hyperbolic caricatures like Martha Dodd, the Tarletons, Birdy Peters, the acned actress, and Jacques La Borwitz (the "mental cadaver"). At points—like Celia's discovery of the naked Birdy Peters in her father's closet—the narrative turns to pure farce.

Though *Last Tycoon* is another in the succession of first-person Southland narratives we have encountered, its first-person narration by Celia Brady is clearly its most serious flaw. Clumsy suppositions and even more awkward omniscience are forced upon her. Fitzgerald's persistence in trying to shape Celia into a credible reporter of the novel's events —and to shape the events to Celia's reach—attests perhaps to the strength of the first-person impulse in Hollywood fiction. But so numerous are the occasions of narrative awkwardness in the novel's first six chapters that they also attest, not just to a need for the technical ironing-out Fitzgerald would have given them, but to a lack of a totally clear perspective upon his materials—the kind of clear perspective that makes Nick Carraway's the indispensable viewpoint of *Gatsby*.

The importance of *eyes* in the novel—a rumor about Pete Zavras's eyes threatens his career; the acne-scarred actress remains a valuable property for the "starlight" in her eyes; Stahr's first encounter with Kathleen is a meeting and tangling of eyes—suggests how centrally important are sight and visuality in Hollywood narrative. Fitzgerald's best pieces of character-building in the stories—Pat's shivering naked in the "Artist's Studio," and Pat as "bit player" who looked "the sort of father who should *never* come home"—are accomplished visually. In the novel, Fitzgerald at times piles metaphor upon metaphor to vivify the narrative:

> [Boxley] knew that Stahr, the helmsman, was finding time
> for him in the middle of a constant stiff blow—that they
> were talking in the always creaking rigging of a ship sail-

ing in great awkward tacks along an open sea. Or else—
it seemed at times—they were in a huge quarry—where
even the newly-cut marble bore the tracery of old pedi-
ments, half-obliterated inscriptions of the past.

The very last of Fitzgerald's notes appended by Edmund
Wilson to the novel is the entry "ACTION IS CHARAC-
TER," an aphorism which could well serve as aesthetic touch-
stone for most Hollywood fiction. As Sidney Fineman in
Schulberg's *Sammy* lectured his uninitiated writer on the
principle, so Stahr lectures Boxley on it twice. Fitzgerald
practices it assiduously. After two opening chapters as a
shadowy, Gatsby-like figure, Stahr comes to light through a
brilliant series of action scenes in chapter three, each flashing
him through one or another of his roles as producer *extraordinaire*. Sergio Perosa goes even further in measuring the impact of Hollywood on Fitzgerald's later prose. He sees an
earlier "involuted style" giving way to "the lightness of one
that is spoken, rapid, and staccato," with Fitzgerald renounc-
ing the ornate word for the effective one, turning his previ-
ously "musical sentences" into terse and direct statements,
and reducing the fullness of his earlier prose to "the scanti-
ness of effects of a movie script." Overstating his case for
The Pat Hobby Stories, Perosa sees genuine achievement in
"the bareness and quickness" of their dialogue.[7] In the novel,
he sees language devoid of syntactical subordination again
breaking constantly into dialogue, with single scenes not
gradually unfolding as before, but now compressed into "significant moments and sudden flashes," with the "kinetic
force" of unencumbered active verbs impelling the narrative
(which technique Perosa demonstrates at length).[8] It is this
dependence upon intensely vivid flashes of action which
causes Michael Millgate to downgrade the novel—notwithstanding its incompleteness—as "a collection of brilliant and
powerful scenes which hardly yet begin to cohere into a
novel." [9] Millgate's criticism of course parallels Comerchero's
displeasure with the narrative technique of *Day of the Locust*.

Both of Fitzgerald's Hollywood books draw heavily upon
regional items for aesthetic effect, though not with equal

effectiveness. The novel draws broadly, while the stories limit their reach to the studio milieu, the technical labyrinth of the sound stage, and movies themselves, especially the silents. Pat's envy of Orson Welles becomes the Chaplinesque image of a crowded street car where the entrance of one man at the rear forces another out in front—"Welles was in; Hobby was out" (recalling the image of the ramming and bulging mob scene in West). Another story, "Homes of the Stars," begins with a sequence straight out of Mack Sennett: a little moustachioed man and a large woman with a small dog in her lap driving up in a chauffeur-driven limousine to ask directions.

Pat, like Sammy Glick, is a name-dropper. Each dropped name is that of some screen luminary in whose reflected glory Pat can for the moment bask, and each heightens the contrast between the glamorous surface of Hollywood and the seedy inner world of industry hangers-on which Pat inhabits. Fitzgerald also drops names in *The Last Tycoon* to contrast the glittering surface with the jungle struggle beneath. As Stahr battles with Brimmer—who looks like Spencer Tracy but "with a stronger face"—at the Trocadero,

> Gary Cooper came in and sat down in a corner with a bunch of men who breathed whenever he did and looked as if they lived off him and weren't budging. A woman across the room looked around and turned out to be Carole Lombard—

The studio lot, whose fictional potential West so successfully exploited, is drawn upon with more restraint in Fitzgerald's novel, yet almost as startlingly. Foreshadowing the collapse of Stahr's kingdom are pieces of African jungle, French châteaux, ocean schooners, and Broadway swirling through the flood the night of the earthquake. In the novel's most vivid tableau, the two unknown girls cling to the head of Siva in the flood until one of them (presumably Kathleen) comes "sliding smoothly down the cheek of the idol" like an isolated teardrop from the eye of the Destroyer. The uncompleted beach house to which Stahr takes Kathleen—"Another house without a roof"—is but an extension of the movie set's imagery of incompleteness and vulnerability.

Beyond studio and stars, Fitzgerald draws like Schulberg on the Beverly Brown Derby as an emblem of Hollywood's decadence and lassitude—a place whose "clients always look as if they'd like to lie down. . . ." He describes urban zoning in Beverly Hills to accentuate the stratification of Hollywood society. And he draws upon the second-floor balcony walkways characteristic of the region's architecture to symbolize the precariousness intrinsic to the movie industry: Brady's offices are "in the old building with the long balconies and iron rails with their suggestion of a perpetual tightrope."

Topography and natural phenomena are also drawn upon in the novel. Airborn in the opening chapter, Stahr analogizes the California mountainscape beneath him with its hidden passes as a way of describing the special intuition that successful men possess; the analogy had been suggested to Fitzgerald by Thalberg himself over lunch during Fitzgerald's first stay in Hollywood a dozen years before. As Hollywood approaches, the multicolored sands of the desert around it suggest its glittering sterility, and "the Mountains of the Frozen Saw slid[ing] under our propellers" its ominousness. The twinkling "warm darkness" of Glendale Airport into which the plane descends connotes, for one thing, as Fitzgerald explains in his notes, Stahr's reverent passion for the great empire which he had built below; and it even more clearly foreshadows death and Stahr's longing for it. Within several pages, Stahr's dead wife Minna is also described as "warm and glowing." The Long Beach earthquake (besides fixing the story in time) is used to suggest the potential for sudden and violent upheaval later realized in the novel. Symbolically, Stahr sleeps through it. One other element of region drawn upon in the novel is the grunion who punctually surface on California beaches to spawn and die at the hands of beachcombers hunting them in the light of full moon. The grunion are, simultaneously, a suggestive reinforcement of the inner-directed and self-reliant Emersonian Negro whom Stahr and Kathleen meet on the beach, and correlatives for West's people who come to California to die—a juxtaposition implying utter hopelessness.

Like Schulberg's *Sammy*, *The Last Tycoon* is also influenced by Hollywood fictions which precede it, especially by West's. The numerous similarities of theme and motif between *Last Tycoon* and *Day of the Locust*—as well as the numerous parallels and junctures in the lives of their authors—have been abundantly demonstrated by David Galloway.[10]

In his foreword to the novel, Edmund Wilson sees Stahr as "inextricably involved with an industry of which he has been one of the creators, . . . its fate . . . implied by his tragedy." [11] Stahr is an isolated genius in a world of mediocrity, one of the very few who "have ever been able to keep the whole equation of pictures in their heads." Apart from his sympathetic portrayal of Stahr, Fitzgerald's outlook on Hollywood and the Southland is brutally negative. The movie industry is one which ignores its old heroes, letting them "slip away into misery eked out with extra work—" It is an industry in which most of the big shots, who control the destinies of flunkies like Pat, are themselves rapacious and stupid philistines. *The Pat Hobby Stories* are dotted with producers like De Tinc, Jack Berners, and Carl Le Vigne, whose names play on famous industry names like De Mille, Jack Warner, and Joseph Levine. It is an industry whose biggest successes are, like Sammy Glick, constantly on the make.

The lowly status of the writer in Hollywood gets special—and bitter—attention from Fitzgerald, that status which would later see Raymond Chandler, having scripted James Cain's *Double Indemnity*, uninvited to the very press conference called to announce his Academy Award nomination for best screenplay. Pat Hobby, of course, is a parody of the Hollywood writer. Celia tells us that she "grew up thinking that writer and secretary were the same, except that a writer usually smelled of cocktails and came more often to meals." The "old writers' building"—at M.G.M. they put it adjacent to a mortuary and called it the "Iron Lung," but there was one on every lot—was "a row of iron maidens left over from silent days and still resounding with the dull moans of cloistered hacks and bums." "You writers," Stahr tells Wylie, "poop out and get all mixed up, and somebody has to come in and straighten you out. . . . You seem to take things so personally, hating people and worshipping them—always thinking people are so important—especially yourselves. You just ask to be kicked around."

The Southland, to Fitzgerald, is enervating and pernicious: "such a slack, soft place," he wrote Gerald Murphy, "that withdrawal is practically a condition of safety. . . . Everywhere there is . . . corruption or indifference." [12] This sense of regional devitalization carries into both fictions, especially *Tycoon*, where Hollywood is a place with "lassitude in plenty," where "young men and women who lived back East in spirit . . . carr[y] on a losing battle against the climate."

In one quantitative sense, *Last Tycoon* is the most regional of the fictions we have examined, for besides reasserting regional themes and motifs, reflecting region in its narrative style, drawing heavily upon regional items, and reflecting a definite outlook upon the region and its central activity, the novel also provides an accurate sociohistorical perspective which none of the others—not even *Sammy*—can match. The novel gives us, as Perosa says, a clear picture of Hollywood film making, in mechanics and in essence, at a particular period of its development. As its scenes unfold, we observe not only plot and character develop, but an industry at work. We see its *modus operandi*, and feel its tensions and pressures. Stahr's lectures to Boxley and his reprimands of his staff provide an excursion into the mind of a superior film-maker.

No overall judgment of the novel save the most reserved and tentative makes much sense. Its narrative is incomplete, and even its "completed" portions would have undergone further polishing and reshaping by Fitzgerald, an agonizing reviser. As it stands, the fragment is neither as weak as the *Times Literary Supplement* thought, seeing it probable "that the final version . . . would have been . . . thoroughly second rate," [13] nor as strong as John Dos Passos felt, calling it "one of those literary fragments that from time to time appear . . . and profoundly influence the course of human events." [14] While some of its flaws, like the premature timing of Stahr's beating at the hands of Brimmer, seem easily correctable, others, like Celia as narrative focus, are major. Nonetheless, as we have it, the novel does reveal the hand of a still-gifted writer, and it abundantly demonstrates the literary craftsman's use of place in his work.

The Pat Hobby Stories, notwithstanding Perosa's defense of Pat as a valiant prisoner in an existential milieu, remain the hastily written ephemera of the same craftsman. Few of the stories possess any plot complexity, nor demonstrate any compensating subtleties of character, theme, or technique. On the contrary, their narrative technique is occasionally quite clumsy, and their exposition, as in "Putative Father," embarrassingly stilted. Their irony, sole *raison d'être* for a number of the stories, is often heavy-handed; plot structures are forced; and circumstances contrived. The underlying premise that Pat was once a first-rate writer is hard to swallow. Even the stories' order of appearance, which Fitzgerald rightly felt important, remains flawed: "Boil Some Water," for example, which appears early in the sequence, would have achieved its desired plaintiveness more effectively had it come further on, after Pat's subservience at the studios was more firmly established. The *Stories* are, in short, hurried fictions which bear the scars of deadline. They are, however, as the chapter has attempted to demonstrate, nonetheless illuminating from our special critical standpoint, that of the relationship between fiction and place.

Afterword

It is tempting at the conclusion of such a study to mark
Q.E.D. to its central hypothesis. The supposition that place
informs fiction in consistent and critically significant ways
has—at least with reference to a single place and time—been
put to the test, and I think demonstrated. There does seem
to be a substantial, albeit supplementary, critical usefulness
in a regional perspective. It is but a single angle of vision,
with the limitations that implies, but a useful angle nonetheless for insights which other critical perspectives may over-
look. What Irving Howe has said of the political novel may
be said of the regional—that it is *any* novel one wishes to
treat as regional, though there would be little reason for
treating all novels that way.[1] With any one work or group of
works, the perspective should seem promising if it is to be
applied. That promise, rather than any discoverable regionality itself, is, I think, what remains detectable by intuition
alone. With the fictions that concerned us here, that promise
was clearly present. And the perspective, once taken, revealed
a genuine aesthetic regionality of many dimensions in that
fiction. The finalities granted the mathematician, however,
are denied the literary critic; in art, even the best of "proofs"
are fraught with inexactitude and must remain tentative. A
different place, a different time, a different critic, introduce
new and elusive variables which necessitate reapplication of
the regional hypothesis.

To be sure, some of the patterns of consistency we have
observed in Southland fiction derive, in part, from extra-

regional influence. Cain's hyperbole, West's irony, Schulberg's tireless moralism, Fitzgerald's lament for the Great American Dream are all as evident in their works outside of Hollywood as those within. As the Depression persisted through the thirties, the collapse of the American Dream became an increasingly attractive theme for many writers. Then too, Prohibition, labor strife, and events in the international political arena had conditioned the literary sensibility in America—if not the sensibilities of all Americans, as West felt—to continuous violence. As Frohock puts it in his *Novel of Violence in America,* the "thirties were the decade of Pretty Boy Floyd and John Dillinger, of Hitler, Mussolini, Franco, and Tojo. Violence was in the air. . . ." [2] It was no localized phenomenon. The theme of sexual abnormality too is more broadly discernible, in time and place throughout American fiction, though hardly so preoccupying a theme as it became in Hollywood-Southland. Still another cause of consistency is the influence of each of the seven writers upon one another. Except for Chandler, whose labors as a screenwriter did not begin until the forties after his early fictional successes, each of the writers—along with others like Saroyan, Meyer Levin, Erskine Caldwell, and Dashiell Hammett—was part of a network of kindred and mutually acquainted creative spirits within the industry. But certainly a writer writing in and about Hollywood is himself as much a regional item as earthquake or sound stage, and as susceptible to aesthetic employment by other writers with a similar focus. Indeed there are unifying influences which are extraregional. Yet too many patterns of consistency and recurrence mark the eight fictions to deny some measure of regional causation. And too many of them are clearly attributable to place to allow our supposing that Hollywood-Southland be unique in its nourishment of literature.

That specific nourishment can also be seen continuing in the decades which follow. Many of the characteristics of Southland fiction in the thirties are traceable in the later ones of Evelyn Waugh, Ben Hecht, Wright Morris, Norman Mailer, Christopher Isherwood, Gavin Lambert, Joan Didion, and Raymond Chandler's heir, Ross MacDonald—albeit with

evolving changes. The dissolving dream which was Hollywood to the earlier writers has its death acknowledged and
taken for granted in the forties and after. The perversities
and unrealities of the place become accepted conventions.
The forties see comic obituaries like Hecht's *I Hate Actors*
(1944) and Waugh's *The Loved One* (1948) (anticipated
by the Huxleyan parody of *After Many a Summer* in 1939).
Comedy gives way in the fifties to the ennui of Mailer's *Deer
Park* (1955) and the nihilist escapism of Morris's Holly-
wooders in *Love Among the Cannibals* (1957). Into the
sixties and seventies, the irony of earlier Southland fiction
gives way to an existential resignation to the region's spiritual
malaise, a resignation prefigured by Horace McCoy. Smog,
drugs, and freeway incessance become new correlatives for
the same old prevailing toxicity, illusoriness, and kinetic
rampancy of the earlier fictions. So consistent, in fact, does
the influence of the Southland continue to be that any writer
seeking to take its measure in fiction runs a great risk of
cliché, a fate that befalls Gavin Lambert's *The Good-by
People* (1971) after his two earlier and more successful Southland efforts, *The Slide Area* (1959) and *Inside Daisy Clover*
(1963). By now, it takes the vitality of a comic picaro like
Daisy, or the psychic disaster area of a Maria Wyeth, Joan
Didion's Southland emblem in *Play It As It Lays* (1970), to
resist the danger in this tendency of Southland elements to
repeat themselves again and again.

The regional hypothesis employed in the foregoing chapters is a sword with two edges. For the literary critic, it opens
insights into separate works and brings to light otherwise
unnoticed and mutually clarifying relationships between
them. (In a work like *Hope of Heaven* it even helps explain
the otherwise inexplicable.) From another standpoint, that
of the student of place (the cultural anthropologist, sociologist, or social historian), the regional hypothesis is equally
useful. But here a warning is necessary to those who would,
on the well-intended advice of many a social scientist, turn
to literature for reliable documentary perspectives. In Harry
Levin's oft-quoted phrase, literature is more often refraction
than reflection of societal reality. The process of integrating

"external" realities into a work of *belles lettres* involves the selection, arrangement, and manipulation of elements for other than documentary purposes. West's climactic riot scene in *Day of the Locust* does not, I think, reflect the social dynamics of mob violence quite so accurately as sociologist Lewis Coser feels,[3] nor is it intended to. Its primary function is that of metaphor; its details are shaped toward that end. There is always present some degree of aesthetic "distortion," making Joyce's Dublin, Faulkner's Mississippi, West's Hollywood, or McCoy's dance marathon not wholly reliable pictures for those who are interested *per se* in Dublin, Mississippi, Hollywood life styles, or the marathon phenomenon. But the student of region, armed with our hypothesis, *can* draw wholly valid assumptions about a place from those discernible patterns of consistency and recurrence that run throughout a regional corpus. That is to say, though writer A, for aesthetic (or polemic) reasons, may portray a skewed reality, when writers B, C, D, and E portray in so many respects the same reality—as Southland writers do—marked not only by the same objective characteristics but the same states of mind, one can with assurance begin to draw inductive insights into the place. That second edge cuts just as well if one uses it wisely. In either respect, the aesthetic or the societal, the regional hypothesis here applied to the fiction of California's Southland, and I think found of value, most surely awaits further application.

Notes

1 — The Regional Perspective and Hollywood-Southland

1. Howard Odum and Harry Estill Moore, *American Regionalism: A Cultural-Historical Approach to National Integration* (New York: Henry Holt, 1938), p. 173.

2. Marjorie Kinnan Rawlings, "Regional Literature of the South," *College English* 1 (1940), 384.

3. Carey M. Williams, *The New Regionalism in America* (Seattle: University of Washington, 1930); Benjamin T. Spencer, "Regionalism in American Literature," in *Regionalism in America*, ed. Merrill Jensen (Madison: University of Wisconsin Press, 1952), chapter 7; Jay Martin, *Harvests of Change: American Literature, 1865–1914* (Englewood Cliffs, N.J.: Prentice-Hall, 1967), chapters 2, 3.

4. Mary Austin, "Regionalism in American Fiction," *English Journal* 21 (1932), 97–107.

5. Frederick Bracher, "California's Literary Regionalism," *American Quarterly* 7 (1955), 277.

6. Donald Davidson, "Regionalism and Nationalism in American Literature," *American Review* 5, no. 1 (1935), 48, 53, 54.

7. Robert Penn Warren, "Some Don'ts for Literary Regionalists," *American Review* 8 (1936), 142–43.

8. Eudora Welty, "Place in Fiction," *South Atlantic Quarterly* 55 (1956), 57–72. Joel Chandler Harris, "Literature in the South," *Atlanta Constitution*, November 30, 1879. An excellent summary of Harris's attitudes on literary sectionalism is contained in Paul M. Cousins, *Joel Chandler Harris* (Baton Rouge: Louisiana State University Press, 1968). Ellen Glasgow, *A Certain Measure* (New York: Harcourt Brace, 1943), p. 67.

9. Scott O'Dell, "An Embarrassing Plenty," *Saturday Review of Literature* 26, no. 44 (October 30, 1943), 5.

10. Quoted in Andrew Turnbull, *Scott Fitzgerald* (New York: Scribner's, 1962), p. 294.

11. Irving Howe, *William Faulkner*, 2nd ed. (New York: Random House, Vintage Books, 1962), p. 42.

12. Carolyn See, *The Hollywood Novel: An Historical and Critical Study* (Ph.D. diss., U.C.L.A., 1963), p. 1.

13. One can, in fact, see in California writing a distinct regional trifurcation, distinguishing between the Olympian misanthropy or disinterestedness of Robinson Jeffers and Walter Van Tilburg Clark, the essential sanguinity and sentimentality of central valley writers like Saroyan and Steinbeck, and the sardonic and skeptical moralism of the more transient Hollywood-Southland writers (which we shall explore). This triple subregionality is ample hypothesis for a separate study, one well beyond the limits of the present one.

2 – The Postman and the Marathon

1. Alonzo Delano, *Life on the Plains and Among the Diggings* (Auburn and Buffalo: Miller, Orton & Mulligan, 1854), p. 349.

2. James M. Cain, *Cain X3* (New York: Knopf, 1969), p. 80. All subsequent references are to this edition.

3. It is informative in examining these questions of identity which recur throughout Southland fiction to look back upon nineteenth-century San Francisco at the profusion of writers who —as protagonists in their own narrative essays, journalistic hoaxes, and social commentary—felt compelled to assume *noms de plume*, sometimes a variety of them: Alonzo Delano ("Old Block"), Louisa Smith ("Dame Shirley"), George Horatio Derby ("John Phoenix"), Bret Harte ("The Bohemian," "Jefferson Brick," "Alexis Puffer"), Sam Clemens ("Mark Twain"), William Wright ("Dan de Quille"), John Rollin Ridge ("Yellow Bird"), Prentice Mulford ("Dogberry"), W. S. Kendall ("Comet Quirls"). Franklin Walker speculates that these writers felt compelled to adopt new personae behind which to observe the faintly unreal milieu of the California Gold Rush. Walker, *San Francisco's Library Frontier* (New York: Knopf, 1939), pp. 29–30.

4. Edwin L. Sabin, "California—Sources and Resources," *Saturday Review of Literature* 26, no. 44 (October 30, 1943), p. 3.

5. Horace McCoy, *They Shoot Horses, Don't They?* (Harmondsworth, England: Penguin Books, 1965), p. 121. All subsequent references are to this edition.

6. David Madden, *James M. Cain* (New York: Twayne, 1970), p. 109.

7. From John Phoenix, "Sandy-Ago-A Soliloquy," cited in Franklin Walker, *A Literary History of Southern California* (Berkeley: University of California Press, 1950), p. 91.

8. Frederick Bracher, "California's Literary Regionalism," *American Quarterly* 7 (1955), 282.

9. Quoted in Jay Martin, *Nathanael West: The Art of his Life* (New York: Farrar, Straus and Giroux, 1970) p. 261.

10. Albert Van Nostrand, *The Denatured Novel* (Indianapolis: Bobbs-Merrill, 1960), p. 126.

11. Cain's preface to *The Butterfly* (New York: Knopf, 1947) pp. x–xi.

12. William Plomer in *The Spectator* 152, (June 8, 1934), 152.

13. Van Nostrand, pp. 126, 127.

14. W. M. Frohock, *The Novel of Violence in America*, 2nd ed. (Dallas: Southern Methodist University Press, 1957), p. 15.

15. Edmund Wilson, "The Boys in the Back Room," *Classics and Commercials* (New York: Farrar, Straus & Co., 1950), p. 20.

16. Thomas Sturak, "Horace McCoy's Objective Lyricism," in *Tough Guy Writers of the Thirties*, ed. David Madden (Carbondale: Southern Illinois University Press, 1968), pp. 161–62.

3 — A Hopeless Southland Allegory

1. Alfred Kazin, *New York Herald Tribune Books*, March 20, 1938, p. 2.

2. Edmund Wilson, *Classics and Commercials* (New York: Farrar, Straus & Co., 1950), p. 24.

3. Sheldon Grebstein, *John O'Hara* (New York: Twayne, 1966), p. 97.

4. Frederick Bracher, "California's Literary Regionalism," *American Quarterly* 7 (1955), 282.

5. John O'Hara, *Hope of Heaven* (London: Panther, 1960), p. 38. All subsequent references are to this edition.

6. Carolyn See, "The Hollywood Novel: The American Dream Cheat," in *Tough Guy Writers of the Thirties*, ed. David Madden (Carbondale: Southern Illinois University Press, 1968), p. 213.

4—Shriek of the Locusts

1. Nathanael West, *The Complete Works of Nathanael West* (New York: Farrar, Straus and Cudahy, 1957), p. 317. All subsequent references are to this edition.

2. Victor Comerchero, *Nathanael West: The Ironic Prophet* (Seattle: University of Washington Press, 1967), pp. 145–48.

3. Randall Reid, *The Fiction of Nathanael West* (Chicago: University of Chicago Press, 1967) pp. 124–30.

4. Nathanael West, "Some Notes on Violence," *Contact* 1 (1932), pp. 132–33.

5. Comerchero, p. 137.

6. Jay Martin, *Nathanael West: The Art of His Life* (New York: Farrar, Straus and Giroux, 1970), p. 333.

7. Martin, *Nathanael West*, p. 304.

8. Comerchero, p. 132.

9. Reid, pp. 121–24.

10. F. Scott Fitzgerald, letter to S. J. Perelman, June 7, 1939, in *The Letters of F. Scott Fitzgerald*, ed. Andrew Turnbull (New York: Scribner's, 1963), pp. 583–84.

11. Reid, p. 152.

12. West, in a letter to Jack Conroy, quoted in Richard Gehman's Introduction to *The Day of the Locust* (New York: New Classics, 1950), pp. ix–x.

13. James Light, *Nathanael West: An Interpretive Study* (Evanston, Ill.: Northwestern University Press, 1961), pp. 175–76.

14. George Milburn, "The Hollywood Nobody Knows," *Saturday Review of Literature* 20 (May 20, 1939), 14–15.

15. Comerchero, p. 131.

16. Martin, *Nathanael West*, p. 340.

17. Allan Seager, letter to Cyril Schneider, April 15, 1952; Quoted in Light, *Nathanael West*, p. 153.

18. Martin, *Nathanael West*, p. 306.

19. Milburn, *Saturday Review of Literature* 20 (May 20, 1939), 14–15.

20. Quoted in Martin, *Nathanael West*, p. 338.

21. Edmund Wilson, *Classics and Commercials* (New York: Farrar, Straus & Co., 1950) pp. 53–54.

5—Grey Knight in the Great Wrong Place

1. Edmund Wilson, *Classics and Commercials* (New York: Farrar, Straus & Co., 1950) pp. 262–63.

2. W. H. Auden, "The Guilty Vicarage," *The Dyer's Hand* (New York: Random House, 1962), p. 151.

3. From Chandler's dedication, to Joseph Thompson Shaw of *Five Murderers* (New York: Avon, 1944).

4. Raymond Chandler, *The Raymond Chandler Omnibus* (New York: Alfred A. Knopf, 1964), p. 287. All subsequent references are to this edition.

5. John Whitley, "Raymond Chandler and the Traditions," *The London Review* 2 (1967) 36.

6. Whitley, p. 34 f. Philip Durham, *Down These Mean Streets A Man Must Go: Raymond Chandler's Knight* (Chapel Hill: University of North Carolina Press, 1963), p. 81.

7. Quoted in Durham, p. 3.

8. *Raymond Chandler Speaking* (Boston: Houghton Mifflin, 1962), pp. 118, 126.

9. Whitley, pp. 35–36.

10. George P. Elliot, "Country Full of Blondes," *The Nation*, April 23, 1960, p. 358.

11. Durham, p. 59.

12. Herbert Ruhm, "Raymond Chandler: From Bloomsbury to the Jungle—and Beyond," in *Tough Guy Writers of the Thirties*, ed. David Madden (Carbondale: Southern Illinois University Press, 1968), p. 174.

13. Norman Rabkin, *Shakespeare and the Common Understanding* (New York: The Free Press, 1967), pp. 59–61.

6—Tycoon Sammy

1. Budd Schulberg, *What Makes Sammy Run?* (New York: Random House, Modern Library Edition, 1952), p. vii. All references to the novel are from this edition.

2. Chester Eisinger, *Fiction of the Forties* (Chicago: University of Chicago Press, 1963), p. 103.

3. Eisinger, p. 103.

7—The Hero and the Hack

1. Fitzgerald in a letter to Arnold Gingrich, June 14, 1940. Quoted in Gingrich, Introduction to *The Pat Hobby Stories* (New York: Scribner's, 1962), p. xviii. References to the *Stories* are from this edition.

2. James E. Miller, *F. Scott Fitzgerald: His Art and His Techniques* (New York University Press, 1964), p. 157.

3. F. Scott Fitzgerald, *The Crack-Up*, ed. Edmund Wilson (New York, New Directions, 1945), p. 109.

4. F. Scott Fitzgerald, *The Last Tycoon* (New York: Scribner's, 1969), p. 21. All subsequent references are to this edition.

5. Maxwell Perkins, in a letter to Fitzgerald, November 30, 1939, published in *Esquire* 75 (June 1971), 182.

6. Fitzgerald, in a letter to Scottie, November 4, 1939, in *The Letters of F. Scott Fitzgerald*, ed. Andrew Turnbull (New York: Scribner's, 1963), p. 63.

7. Sergio Perosa, *The Art of F. Scott Fitzgerald*, trans. Charles Matz and Perosa, (Ann Arbor: University of Michigan Press, 1965), p. 151.

8. Perosa, pp. 174–76.

9. Michael Millgate, "Scott Fitzgerald as a Social Novelist: Statement and Technique in *The Last Tycoon*," *English Studies* 43 (1962), 29–34.

10. David Galloway, "Nathanael West's Dream Dump," *Critique* 6 (1963), 61–63.

11. Edmund Wilson, Foreword to *The Last Tycoon* (New York: Scribner's, 1941), p. x.

12. Fitzgerald, in a letter to Gerald Murphy, Sept. 14, 1940, *Letters*, pp. 429–30.

13. *Times Literary Supplement*, no. 2503 (January 20, 1950), p. 40.

14. John Dos Passos, "A Note on Fitzgerald," in *The Crack-Up*, p. 339.

Afterword

1. Irving Howe, *Politics and the Novel* (New York: Fawcett, 1967), p. 18.

2. W. M. Frohock, *The Novel of Violence in America* (Dallas: Southern Methodist University Press, 1957), p. 13.

3. Lewis Coser, *Sociology Through Literature* (Englewood Cliffs, N.J.: Prentice-Hall, 1963), p. 5.

Bibliographical Note

Southland fiction as such, embracing the Hollywood novel and other "tough guy" fictions on the Hollywood periphery, gets its first book-length treatment in this study. Edmund Wilson s 1940 essay, "The Boys in the Back Room," in *Classics and Commercials* (New York: Farrar, Straus & Co., 1950) is the earliest and best-known look at southern California writers as a group. Frederick Bracher, "California's Literary Regionalism," *American Quarterly* 7, no. 3 (Fall 1955) briefly examines the same writers and their thematic and technical relationships to other California writers and the larger literary region of California. The Hollywood genre is the subject of a recent book by Jonas Spatz, *Hollywood in Fiction: Some Versions of the American Myth* (The Hague and Paris: Mouton, 1969); and Carolyn See's unpublished, but oft-alluded-to, encyclopedic, and perceptive dissertation, "The Hollywood Novel: An Historical and Critical Study" (U.C.L.A., 1963). David Madden, ed., *Tough Guy Writers of the Nineteen Thirties* (Carbondale: Southern Illinois University Press, 1968) is the best single source of critical approaches to the "tough guy" genre; it also includes a useful essay by Miss See, "The Hollywood Novel: The American Dream Cheat." Indispensable for historical backgrounds to modern California literature are Franklin Walker's two superb studies, *San Francisco's Literary Frontier* (New York: Knopf, 1939) and *A Literary History of Southern California* (Berkeley: University of California Press, 1950).

The best historical studies of the idea of literary regionalism in America are Benjamin T. Spencer, "Regionalism in American Literature," in *Regionalism in America*, ed. Merrill Jensen (Madison: University of Wisconsin Press, 1952); Jay Martin's chronologically narrower but insightful chapters (2 and 3) on regionalism in *Harvests of Change: American Literature 1865–1914* (Englewood Cliffs, N.J.: Prentice-Hall, 1967); and Carey McWilliams's analysis of regionalism's various manifestations in the 1920s, *The New Regionalism in American Literature* (Seattle: University of Washington, 1930).

On James M. Cain, the most important study to date is David Madden's recent *James M. Cain* (New York: Twayne, 1970). Madden's *Tough Guy Writers* volume contains a useful essay by the novelist Joyce Carol Oates, "Man Under Sentence of Death: The Novels of James M. Cain." Also of interest are the treatments of *Postman* in Albert Van Nostrand, *The Denatured Novel* (Indianapolis: Bobbs-Merrill, 1960); and W. M. Frohock, *The Novel of Violence in America* (Dallas: Southern Methodist University, 1957).

On Horace McCoy there is, as yet, little available. Edmund Wilson treats him perfunctorily in "The Boys in the Back Room." Only Thomas Sturak's essay, "Horace McCoy's Objective Lyricism," in Madden's *Tough Guy Writers*, and Sturak's unpublished Ph.D. dissertation, "The Life and Writings of Horace McCoy" (U.C.L.A., 1967), do justice to this significant minor writer. Lee J. Richmond, "A Time to Mourn and a Time to Dance," *Twentieth Century Literature* 17, no. 2 (1971) offers some expansion on the theme of existential estrangement already treated by Sturak.

Slow in getting started, the critical literature on O'Hara has begun to grow. *Hope of Heaven*, however, receives little of its attention, being generally dismissed as utter failure.

The critical literature on Nathanael West also grows after a slow start, in West's case in belated recognition of imaginative genius. Biographically, Jay Martin's recent work, *Nathanael West: The Art of His Life* (New York: Farrar, Straus and Giroux, 1970) is superb; it will stand as definitive for many years. Critically, the best treatments of West are Stanley Edgar Hyman, *Nathanael West* (Minneapolis: University of Minnesota Pamphlets on American Writers, no. 21, 1962); Victor Comerchero, *Nathanael West: The Ironic Prophet* (Seattle: University of Washington Press, 1967); and Randall Reid, *The Fiction of Nathanael West* (Chicago: University of Chicago Press, 1967). James Light's pioneering work on West, *Nathanael West: An Interpretive Study* (Evanston: Northwestern University Press, 1961) remains useful. A new treatment of West's fiction by Irving Malin, *Nathanael West's Novels* (Carbondale: Southern Illinois University Press, 1972) has arrived too late for consideration under the pressures of my own deadline.

The most valuable background study of Raymond Chandler is Philip Durham, *Down These Mean Streets A Man Must Go: Raymond Chandler's Knight* (Chapel Hill: University of North Carolina Press, 1963). On Chandler's place in the detective-story tradition, John Whitley's essay, "Raymond Chandler and the Traditions," *London Review* 2 (August 1967) is extremely perceptive. Useful, too, are Herbert Ruhm, "Raymond Chandler: From Bloomsbury to the Jungle—and Beyond," in Madden's *Tough Guy Writers*; and (though he curiously neglects *Farewell, My Lovely*) George P. Elliot, "Country Full of Blondes," *Nation*, April 23, 1960.

Budd Schulberg has received little critical attention to date. Chester Eisinger's disparagement, in his *Fiction of the Forties* (Chicago: University of Chicago Press, 1963), of Schulberg's "old fashioned liberalism" is fairly typical in its response to Sammy's creator.

Fitzgerald, of course, has elicited a voluminous critical literature, a substantial portion of it focused upon the uncompleted *Last Tycoon*. *Pat Hobby*, however, has received very little of this attention. Specifically useful on Fitzgerald in Hollywood are Jonas Spatz, "Fitzgerald, Hollywood and the Myth of Success," in Warren French, ed., *The Thirties* (De Land, Fla.: Everett/ Edwards, 1967); and Aaron Latham's recent study of Fitzgerald as a screenwriter, *Crazy Sundays* (New York: Viking, 1971).

Index